CW00550036

Corporal Brown's Campaigns in the Low Countries

A Grenadier Company Sergeant

Corporal Brown's Campaigns in the Low Countries

Recollections of a Coldstream Guard
in the Early Campaigns Against
Revolutionary France 1793–1795

Robert Brown

LEONAUR

Corporal Brown's Campaigns in the Low Countries: Recollections of a Coldstream Guard in the Early Campaigns Against Revolutionary France 1793-1795
by Robert Brown

First published in 1795 under the title
*An Impartial Journal of a Detachment From the Brigade of Foot Guards,
Commencing 20th February 1793 and Ending 9th May 1795*

The introduction 'The Fight With Revolutionary France'
has been adapted from *A Short History of the British Army to 1914*
by Eric William Shepherd

Published by Leonaur Ltd

This version of the original text has been specially prepared for Leonaur
by Frederick Llewellyn, to whom the publishers would like to express their
thanks, and with material original to this edition is
copyright © 2008 Leonaur Ltd

ISBN: 978-1-84677-490-4 (hardcover)
ISBN: 978-1-84677-489-8 (softcover)

http://www.leonaur.com

Publisher's Notes

The opinions expressed in this book are those of the author
and are not necessarily those of the publisher.

Contents

The Fight With Revolutionary France

Within six short years of the triumph of France over Great Britain in the world contest arising out of the American rebellion, Nemesis had overtaken her incompetent and bankrupt monarchy, and the whole country was plunged into the throes of revolution. The course of that Revolution, wherein were laid the foundations of modern France and modern Europe, followed the usual road—from a limitation of the absolute powers of the Crown to the abolition first of these powers, then of the Crown itself; from government by elected assembly to mob rule, and thence to the unfettered power of a self-appointed oligarchy—a road as old as Greece, as new as Russia. From the military point of view, with which alone we are concerned, the Revolution heralded the first appearance of a new phenomenon—the nation in arms, and the complete supersession of eighteenth-century warfare by the strategic and tactical methods of our own day. The Revolutionary and Napoleonic epochs mark the beginning of modern military history. For the British army, in fine, they form the last and most bitterly contested of the long series of conflicts with France, which cover more than five centuries of our country's story, and the establishment of our national independence and the acquisition of our overseas empire. In these twenty odd years, from 1793 to

1815, the army underwent its sternest and most searching test in a struggle which, until a yet greater war came in our own time to rob it of the title, was justly termed the Great War.

That war was not entered upon lightly or easily. For a period of ten years, subsequent to the Peace of Versailles, England, under the prudent leadership of William Pitt, the son of the great Chatham, held aloof from all European entanglements, and devoted her energies to the restoration of her stability and economic prosperity. She held aloof from the Royalist crusade which in 1792, on the news of the dethronement of the House of Bourbon in France, set forth under the leadership of Austria and Prussia to repress the Revolution by armed force, and impassively watched the defeat of the invaders. Neither the Government nor the people, however, could see unmoved the violent course of the dominant faction in Paris, the tyranny and blood-lust of the Jacobins, or the doctrines, subversive alike of liberty and order, which French arms were to propagate wherever their career of conquest should carry them, imposing them by force on unwilling peoples. None the less, it was only when the Revolutionary armies, gathering in strength on their northern frontier, menaced the independence of the Low Countries, ever England's predominant Continental interest, that the latter felt herself compelled to have recourse to arms, and ally with Austria, Russia, the lesser states of Germany, Spain and Holland against the common enemy of Europe.

Thus the British army in the first months of 1793 found itself once more preparing for active service. Its constitution and government had been considerably remodelled during the previous ten years of peace; by the provisions of Burke's Act of 1783, all matters of recruitment and finance, hitherto the concern only of the regimental commanders, had been taken over by the Government, which had also reorganised the command and administration of the army under two newly appointed heads, the secretary of state for war and the commander-in-chief. The peace strength had now sunk to its normal level of 17,000 men, and steps were at once taken to increase it, first by the method adopted during the American War, of purchasing from Hanover and Hesse the services of 20,000 mercenaries, and then by the raising of a number of new regiments of Horse and Foot (some 37,000 in all). By these measures an adequate field army would be provided, while for purposes of home defence the militia was largely increased, recruiting by ballot being instituted in 1794, and two additional forces, known respectively as Fencibles and Volunteers, were also raised for the same purpose. As the result of these measures the establishments by the end of 1794 showed a sum total of 75,000 British regulars and mercenaries, and 90,000 home defence troops, in all 165,000 men under arms. Imposing as these figures were, they might have been largely increased by the elimination of competition for eligible men between the various arms and forces, and the institution of one regular, economical and efficient recruiting system for the whole of the armed forces of the Crown. Moreover, the physical and military qualities of both officers and men left much to be desired; training and fighting methods were out of date; armament, clothing and equipment were inadequate; and the system of transport and supply, only recently reorganised on a sound basis, was, as yet, inelastic and uncertain in its working. Altogether the British fighting machine was well below the standard even of the Continental armies of its day, and as yet by no means fit for the arduous tasks which the coming campaigns were to impose upon it.

Such being the weapon at his disposal, Pitt had now to consider how to use it. His main idea was to employ the army in cooperation with the navy against the overseas trade and possessions of France; such had been its role in recent wars, and in this case the historical argument was fortified by what appeared to be common sense. Pitt believed that Revolutionary France financially and economically was at her last gasp, and that sheer exhaustion must shortly compel her to lay down her arms; the capture of her few remaining colonies must tend to hasten this desirable consummation, besides being of direct advantage to Britain. The revolt in the French West Indian Islands, which broke out a few months previous to the commencement of the war, seemed to offer a golden opportunity for applying this policy with rapidity and effect, and the main strength of the British regular army was therefore despatched with all possible speed to that sphere of operations. At the same time our interests in the Low Countries could not be entirely neglected, and it was decided also to send a contingent to co-operate with the Allied armies in that theatre.

Such was Pitt's initial plan. Various small expeditions were despatched against other distant overseas objectives; home defence became more and more a matter of pressing concern; and a series of attempts were made to foment or assist by armed force risings against the Revolutionary Government in the disaffected coastal districts of France. Under these conditions our military operations tended to become incoherent and wasteful, and all the more difficult to describe clearly and succinctly because of the non-existence of any consistent and logical general plan underlying the whole. These included the following five principal campaigns: (1) The Campaign in the Low Countries, 1793-1795; (2) the West Indies Operations, 1793-1800; (3) Minor Operations in Europe and elsewhere (the Mediterranean, the French coasts, Ireland, the Cape, etc.), 1793-1798; (4) the Expedition to North Holland, 1799; (5) the Egyptian Expedition, 1800.

THE CAMPAIGN IN THE LOW COUNTRIES—1793-1795

The various powers composing the First Coalition were, when England added herself to their number, anything but a happy family. The two greatest, Austria and Prussia, were consumed by mutual distrust and jealousy over the question of the fate of Poland; Spain, Sardinia and the minor German states were weak and corrupt; and Holland was apathetic, one might almost say disaffected towards the common cause. At the opening of the campaign of 1793 the Allied armies in the Netherlands, comprising in all some 60,000 men, were drawn up along the southern frontier, with their main strength north of Valenciennes, in face of that of the enemy entrenched in a position covering that fortress. The French army, weaker in numbers and under a divided command, was widely dispersed along a line from the Sambre on the right to Dunkirk on the left in an attempt to cover every possible avenue of invasion open to the Allies, who, on their part, were little less scattered. The latter possessed a fighting machine undoubtedly superior to that of their adversaries, but the methods of making war held in honour among them were such as to preclude any serious attempt to exploit this advantage; their leaders could conceive of nothing beyond a steady and methodical advance through the fortress barrier guarding the approaches to the heart of France, and a strict limitation of the objectives of each successive step. This strategy played into the hands of their adversaries by granting them the needed respite to restore their armies to the high standard of efficiency attained before the Revolution came to ruin discipline and undermine morale.

The forces in British pay, numbering in all 27,000, of whom at the outset some 20,000 were German mercenaries, arrived at Tournai in April, the Duke of York being in chief command. Coburg, the Austrian generalissimo, had already drawn up his plan of campaign, which involved an advance of the main army against the French entrenched camp before Valenciennes, the flanking of the fortress barrier at that point, and the capture of the strong places to the east of it. Once these preliminaries had been accomplished a decisive advance on Paris might be safely undertaken, and in any case the Allies would have gained real advantages. Unfortunately, the British Government felt the need of acquiring some tangible gain which it might present to its people as an early and adequate result of our military effort in the Netherlands, and in an evil hour it was agreed that after the capture of Valenciennes, the British contingent should be permitted to possess itself of Dunkirk.

This ill-advised decision went far to ruin what might well have been the decisive campaign of 1793. The first part of the programme was carried out without a hitch; the French entrenched camp was carried by storm, the fortress of Valenciennes invested and compelled to capitulate, and the hostile army forced back across the upper Scheldt. Then, with some four months of good campaigning weather still before them the Allies divided their forces and went their several ways as arranged— Coburg to besiege Maubeuge, York to secure Dunkirk. The latter found the task too great for his resources: the necessary naval cooperation was unduly delayed, his siege artillery was inadequate, and his forces were too small even to permit of a complete investment of the place. The French thus had ample time to despatch an army to its rescue; advancing from the south, it defeated and drove off at Hondschoote the troops detailed to cover the siege, and compelled York to abandon his heavy guns and fall back in haste for fear of being cut off from his base at Ostend. He effected his retreat in safety, largely because his enemies had turned their attention to Coburg, who was in his turn compelled by the French victory of Wattignies to raise the siege of Maubeuge. York was not only too far away to be able to arrive in time to be of use, but his eastward march was interrupted by the news of a French diversion which caused anxiety for the security of Flanders and compelled him to retrace his steps. The operations thus came to an end with the apparent advantage indeed on the side of the Allies; but in actual fact they had by their dilatoriness and divided counsels lost their best chance of decisively defeating their adversaries while still weak.

For by the beginning of next year there was no prospect of the Allies being able successfully to execute their proposed plan for an advance on Paris. Their mutual mistrust was becoming more rather than less acute with the lapse of time; the condition of their troops was going from bad to worse, and their effectives were gradually diminishing, so that to the 240,000 French under Pichegru and Jourdan who stood arrayed between the Moselle and the sea, they could oppose barely half that number, though these were still superior to their enemies in all military qualities. The main army, with which was the Duke of York's British contingent of 22,000 men, was again assembled around Valenciennes, preparing to advance against the centre of the French host, which on its side was planning a double enveloping movement against both the Allied flanks by way of Ghent and Liege. In April, however, Coburg took the initiative, attacking Pichegru in his fortified position between Cambrai and Le Cateau and forcing him to retire towards Guise. Siege was then laid to Landrecies, and the French attempts at relief were beaten off in two brilliant little actions in which the British cavalry covered themselves with glory. Accordingly Pichegru determined to try the effect of a diversion in Flanders, where his progress rapidly became so menacing that York was sent hurriedly to the rescue, to be followed soon after by the main body of the army. In the two days' battle of Tourcoing lack of cohesion and bad staff work threw away the results of the first successful British advance and exposed the victorious troops to annihilating attacks on both flanks, from which they were only extricated after heavy losses. Following his success, Pichegru once more assailed the right of the Allied line, while Jourdan in the Sambre valley pressed back their left, thus forcing Coburg in his anxiety for his communications to hasten eastwards, leaving York at Tournai to make what head he could against the very superior numbers of the enemy. British reinforcements arrived at Ostend only to become involved in the general retreat, which led the Allied troops in two months back by way of the Scheldt valley,

Malines and Antwerp to the Dutch frontier, while Coburg, defeated at Fleurus, was compelled to retire down the Meuse and sever his connection with his Allies.

The Duke of York was thus left to secure the inviolability of Holland with 25,000 ill-trained, ill-equipped and ill-clothed troops whose officers were inferior and whose morale was declining. No assistance could be expected from the Dutch, and there was no prospect that the defensive front of close on 100 miles on the north bank of the Meuse between Venloo and the head of the estuary could be held against any serious attack. The continued retirement of the Austrians uncovered the Duke's left, and Pichegru, by a combined front and flank attack, compelled him to fall back behind the Waal. Winter had now set in; operations came to an end and the British commander left for England, handing over the charge of the army to the Hanoverian, Walmoden. But the intense cold quickly froze the waters of the river which separated the opposing forces, and Pichegru seized his opportunity to force the passage, first of the Waal, and then of the Leek, overrun Holland, and seize the Dutch fleet lying helpless in the Texel. The British army, falling back north-eastwards to the Yssel and the Ems under conditions which were a foretaste, on a smaller scale, of those of the retreat from Moscow, was for all practical purposes dissolved as a fighting force before, in April 1795, it finally reached its transports at Bremen.

So ended in utter disaster one of the few really discreditable episodes in our army's history. None the less, though the Duke of York had conclusively proved himself unequal to a high command in the field; though among both officers and troops almost every military quality was conspicuous by its absence, and the sole redeeming feature throughout remained the fighting value of the troops in battle, the main responsibility for the disaster must lie on the shoulders of the Government and people of England, who sent overseas an army unfitted for its work, neglected to provide it with the first essentials for success, and finally left it to starve and freeze for want of the bare necessities of existence. Not for the first time nor for the last had the luckless British army to serve as a scapegoat for the country's lack of preparedness and military inefficiency.

To Major-General Lake

Sir, The very high honour that you have conferred by permitting me to dedicate the following work to a gentleman and a general of your great and well-known abilities, will always command my most grateful acknowledgements, as under such a protector the numerous imperfections therein contained will be the more readily excused. To you, sir, as our first commander under His Royal Highness the Duke of York, we have been long taught to pay the most cheerful obedience; but we can with the greatest propriety and justice say more, namely, that such obedience was not paid to you merely as a General, and our commander, but as our father; not only to one whose authority extended over our persons, but to one who possessed our warmest affections; to one whose presence never failed to infuse with an irresistible power, a spirit of cheerfulness and ardour into every heart: every hardship was despised, while we beheld you sharing it with us; and no danger, in whatever shape it might appear, was dreaded while you were our leader. The joyful acclamations with which you were received after a short absence at Courtray; and the pleasure and satisfaction which evinced itself publicly, on every similar occasion, throughout the brigade, may prevent the smallest degree of adulation from being imputed to so humble an individual as, sir, with the greatest respect, your most obliged, most obedient and most devoted humble Servant,
Robert Brown
Windsor,
September, 1795

Preface

The following pages being originally written for my own private amusement, were never intended to meet the public eye, until some time after the brigade returned to England, when, at the instance of a number of my friends, I was induced, at length, to submit them to the press.

As there is a kind of secret pleasure in contemplating past scenes of danger and distress, when the mind is at rest and quiet, this small tract may be acceptable to many of those who shared in the troubles therein described, as it will bring to their remembrance a number of incidents which they had probably forgot. To others, it may serve to correct the wide misrepresentations that have been industriously circulated, either through ignorance or prejudice; for however some may boast of the veracity of their information, yet those who were present in the scenes of action are the best able to judge of the correctness of such a performance.

I have taken notice, as often as opportunity offered, of every other regiment or corps in the British army who were engaged in any particular action; at the same time many circumstances may have occurred among them worthy of remark, which, on account of their distance and my private situation I could not possibly come at the knowledge of. The names of the several posts we occupied, and the time of taking or leaving them, may be depended upon.

The reader is not to expect to find here the eloquent productions of learning, nor the glowing effusions of fancy; but a plain, simple narrative of facts, which were generally minuted down on the evening of the day on which they took place, or the first opportunity afterwards.

All party influence is totally excluded. No circumstance whatever is concealed to favour the one, nor aggravated to please the other; but are, according to the information collected on the spot, related precisely as they took place.

Windsor

September 19th, 1795

CHAPTER 1
February 1793

About this time, the French army under the command of General Dumourier, spreading their baneful influence, as well as their arms, over all West Flanders, into which they found very easy admission, proceeded with rapid strides towards Holland, the invasion of which Dumourier had openly avowed.

His Majesty being bound by a defensive treaty of alliance, was under the necessity of sending a number of troops to assist the Dutch against the common enemy, whose principles and secret combinations, as well as outward profession, militated against every government in Europe.

20th February—Orders were issued that the three first battalions of foot guards should hold themselves in readiness to embark for foreign service. The companies were by the first augmentation to consist of four sergeants, four corporals, two drummers, and seventy-one privates.

23rd February—It not being found convenient to complete the companies to the first establishment, it was ordered that the number of privates should be fifty-six.

24th February—His Royal Highness the Duke of Gloucester ordered that the brigade commanded for foreign service, should be ready to march from the Parade in St. James' Park the next morning at six o'clock, to Greenwich, in order to embark on board the transports provided for that purpose.

His Majesty having appointed his Royal Highness the Duke of York commander in chief of the British forces for foreign service, Major-General Lake was appointed to command the brigade of guards.

25th February—The brigade paraded in the Park, and after being reviewed by his Majesty, marched to Greenwich, and embarked from the hospital stairs. His Majesty was present at the embarkation.

This detachment consisted now of four battalions, the grenadier companies, *viz.* two from the first regiment, and one from each of the others, being formed into a separate battalion, under the command of Colonel Leigh of the 3rd regiment.

26th February—Weighed anchor and dropped down the river to the Nore.

27th February—Remained at anchor.

Weighed anchor and put to sea, under the convoy of two frigates, *viz.* the *Lizard*, Captain Williams, and the *Racehorse*, Captain ——.

CHAPTER 2

March 1793

1st March—Early in the morning a strong gale of wind came on, and the first land we discovered was a point a little to the north of Helvoetsluys; about 9 o'clock a Dutch pilot came on board, and advised our captain to stand a little to the southward; which advice he following, instead of anchoring in a safe and commodious place, run the ship upon a lee more, the wind blowing very strong upon the land.

4th March—Having got all things in readiness, the 3rd regiment disembarked about noon, at Helvoetsluys, where they remained some time, and at Brill; the rest of the brigade going on board of scouts, in order to proceed by water to Dort.

5th March—Proceeded up the river Maese; this country is almost all covered with water, and banks are raised for foot passengers along the sides of the river and canals.

6th March—Arrived at Dort, which is an exceeding beautiful town; it is about three miles in circumference, but of no great strength, there being no works to defend it. Canals are cut all through the town, on which the shipping go to any part of it, The streets are regular and kept remarkably clean, as well as the outside of their houses, which they are continually washing.

But if we were struck with the neat appearance and cleanliness of the streets, and outside of the houses, we were much more so upon seeing the inside, where every article of furniture, whether for use or ornament, is kept in a state of cleanliness and regularity far exceeding any thing we have been accustomed to see in England. The country round the town is very pleasant, being covered with gentlemen's seats and delightful gardens, watered by small rivulets cut from the rivers, and canals.

Two fine yachts were moored here, on board of which the Duke of York and the Prince of Orange slept.

Three companies of the 3rd regiment, after disembarking marched to Brill, and four companies to Helvoet, where they remained till the 25th, when they were relieved by the 14th foot, and set off to join the brigade.

Brill is a very beautiful and strong fortress, surrounded with strong ramparts and a deep wet ditch; there are upwards of 100 pieces of ordnance mounted upon the several batteries. Canals are cut from the river, which spread themselves in branches through different parts of the town.

27th March—In consequence of an order of his, Royal Highness, the commander in chief, the brigade commenced drawing bread in *lieu* of bread money; one pound and a half each man per day. Provisions of every kind are remarkably cheap here, and the inhabitants show a great deal of kindness and respect for our army in general.

30th March—A light company was formed from the brigade, and put under the command of Lieut. Col. Perryn, but attached to the grenadier battalion, which was now called the flank battalion, and consisted of five companies.

The brigade of guards, with a detachment of artillery, received orders to hold themselves in readiness to embark, with all their baggage, etc. on Monday morning next at day-break.

His Royal Highness was pleased to make a present of six pounds of beef for each man, being provision for four days.

Chapter 3
April 1793

1st April—The brigade, except four companies of the 3rd regiment embarked for Bergen-op-Zoom, which four companies followed five days after.

In sailing for Bergen-op-Zoom we passed close under Williamstadt, which place the enemy had laid siege to, but retreated some time before.

Bergen-op-Zoom is thought to be as strong a fortification as any in Europe; besides the great strength of its works, and the vast command it has of the water, being the principal quay of the river Scheldt, it is remarkable for its strong and extensive bomb-proofs, which are said to be capable of containing 100,000 men. The town itself is but inconsiderable, though the works extend about three miles in circumference; the garrison consisted of Dutch troops, the British were quartered in the town.

9th April—About two o'clock in the morning the brigade received orders to embark, and proceed with all possible expedition to Antwerp; the artillery to proceed by land. Accordingly, the men and baggage being embarked, we set sail up the river, and about two o'clock p. m. cast anchor in sight of Antwerp.

A considerable fleet of Dutch and English men of war, with frigates, gunboats, etc. lay in the river; and as we sailed through them they saluted his Royal Highness, as also some batteries on the river side.

10th April—About two o'clock p. m. we landed on the west side of the river, Antwerp being on the east side; and, after receiving two days biscuit, marched about three o'clock, and passed the 53rd and 37th regiments in cantonments; about six o'clock arrived at Bovern, where we were quartered forty or fifty in a house.

The face of this country appears very different from Holland; instead of vast sheets of water and marshy ground, we beheld a country covered with universal verdure, in woods and fields beautifully variegated.

12th April—Halted.

13th April—Marched at seven o'clock in the morning, our column consisted of the brigade of guards, and that of the line, with the artillery, and arrived at Lokeron, a considerable town on the river Durme, ten miles from Ghent. This day we passed through St. Nicholas, on the main road from Antwerp to Ghent, containing a great number of schools for youth of both sexes; two roads cross each other in the centre of the town, and on each road, before you approach the centre a considerable way, the houses, which are very elegant, divide, and form a vast circle, which has a very magnificent appearance.

14th April—Marched at seven o'clock, and arrived at Ghent at one p. m.

This day our attention was engaged by a great number of small buildings, differing very much both in size and elegance, erected at almost every cross-road, or place particularly conspicuous, wherein is set up either a crucifix, or an image of the Virgin with her Son in her arms, but chiefly the latter; at which places all solitary passengers pay their devotions, and at some is an iron box for the reception of their charity.

Ghent is a large town, upwards of eight miles in circumference, situated on the river Scheldt; and also the Lys, which latter loses itself in a number of canals, branching out to the north and west.

There are some remains of a wall and ditch in some places here, and also of a citadel; but it never was of any great strength, and is now in a state of total decay. Some of the churches are very large, and contain some paintings of considerable reputation.

The barracks of St. Peter's are the most commodious we have yet seen, forming an ample square, with piazzas and a gallery all round; the rooms above and below being fitted up for the accommodation of eight men each, the whole being able to contain about 1600 men.

Our troops were quartered in the town, and the people behaved very kind to us.

15th April—Halted.

16th April—This morning the army, having got on board different scouts, proceeded up the canal to Bruges. It snowed very much during our passage, which, crowded as we were, made it very disagreeable.

17th April—Landed at Bruges about seven o'clock in the morning. This is a fine little town, and has a brisk trade by means of its vicinity to Ostend. Provisions of every kind very reasonable. Some small remains of a fortification appear round the town, but no care is taken of it, nor any guns mounted.

18th April—Halted.

19th April—Marched at one in the morning for Thiel, at

which place we arrived about ten in the evening; quartered in the town.

The face of this country is very pleasant, abounding with fir trees.

20th April—Marched at ten o'clock in the morning, and about five o'clock p. m. arrived at Courtray, distance about sixteen miles; country very pleasant and fruitful.

Courtray is a fine populous town, situated on the river Lys; a kind of a mud wall and wet ditch, of no consequence, is all the defence it has: the enemy evacuated this town just before we entered, as they did most of the places we lately passed. The country here is more open and free from wood, though the soil is very rich and produces fine crops. There is no remarkable building in this town; the market-place is confused and irregular, a building of several houses standing in the middle of it. This town forms the northern point of a triangle with Tournay and Lille.

23rd April—Marched at seven o'clock a. m. and about four p. m. arrived at Tournay.

Tournay is a large populous town, defended by an ancient stone wall and a ditch; the citadel is well situated by nature, and was esteemed a masterpiece of art; but this, as well as the rest of the fortifications, is in a state of decay.

This is one of the principal magazines for the British army, on account of the easy navigation of the Scheldt.

The great church here is finely ornamented with marble, and very fine sculpture, though but few paintings of any considerable merit. The several ornaments and vessels pertaining to their worship here are very rich, and have a splendid appearance, which to us, whose mode of worship consists less in external grandeur, appears new, and is viewed with no small degree of curiosity.

25th April—This day we removed our quarters from Tournay to the village of Orcq, about two miles on the Lille road, at which place we were cantoned in barns, or as the situation of the place would permit; the enemy's advanced posts coming within five miles of Tournay, a camp of Austrian cavalry and Prussian infantry laying a little on our left.

29th April—A great number of Hanoverian cavalry arrived at Tournay, under the command of Prince Ernest Augustus, brother to our Royal Duke.

30th April—This day a considerable number of Hanoverian infantry arrived.

Chapter 4

May 1793

1st May—About midnight the army was ordered under arms, and it was thought some sudden attack was to be made; but in consequence of the wetness of the night, and badness of the roads, we returned again about two o'clock this morning.

This afternoon the Prussians struck their tents and marched off; a heavy cannonade was heard all day, which was supposed to be the allies investing Conde.

2nd May—A smart skirmish took place early this morning, between some Austrian cavalry and the enemy, wherein the former had the advantage.

Three regiments of Hanoverian cavalry came from Tournay, and encamped behind our cantonments.

Several skirmishes took place every day between the advanced piquet's, but of no consequence.

8th May—The enemy having strongly entrenched themselves in the woods of St. Amand, reinforced by the greatest part of General Dampier's army, which had been encamped at the strong post of Famars, made a general attack on General Clairfait's posts at the abbey of Vicogne and the wood of St. Amand, but were repulsed with great loss.

The Austrians and Prussians having sustained the first attack, the British, under the command of the Duke of York, marched about one o'clock this morning, as a reserve, till we arrived at the Prussian camp at Maulde, where, we halted a considerable time. The action was now become general, from Conde to the Scarpe, and a dreadful cannonade was heard from every quarter. After we had halted some time, we advanced through, the town of St. Amand, on the *chaussee*, to Valenciennes, the Coldstream battalion being advanced a considerable time before us to reinforce the Prussians. The flank battalion soon after was ordered for the same purpose to another place. The two remaining battalions no sooner had passed through the town, than they met a great number of wounded, both of the Prussians and Coldstream; that battalion having suffered considerably, being led up against a battery, and then forced to abandon it. Ensign Howard, of the Coldstream, who carried the colours, and a sergeant-major and two sergeants, were wounded, and seventy-three rank and file killed, wounded, and missing.

This was the first time the British guards were engaged, and by their courage and intrepidity gained a considerable share in the glory of that day, when the enemy was totally routed, and took refuge at their strong camp at Famars.

The Austrians had upwards of 500 killed and wounded, and the Prussians 300.

9th May—About seven o'clock this morning, we advanced a considerable way towards the enemy, who had not yet left the wood: we halted some time near the Abbey Vicogne, we then returned towards St. Amand, and lay on the road that night.

10th May—Early this morning, the Austrians and Prussians attacked the rear of the flying Carmagnols; soon after which we had intelligence that the enemy had been drove entirely off with great slaughter, and a number taken prisoners. We were ordered to return to our cantonments where we arrived this evening.

12th May—This day we fired a *feu de joie* on account of our late victories.

14th May—A considerable number of English light cavalry arrived at Tournay.

18th May—Received orders to march the next morning at six o'clock.

19th May—Marched at six o'clock through Tournay, on the road towards Valenciennes; and about twelve o'clock arrived at a small village called Briuelle, where we were quartered two or three companies at a house. Our column consisted of the brigade of foot guards, the 14th, 37th, and 53rd regiments, and a great number of Hanoverian infantry. The Hanoverian and British light cavalry covered our rear.

20th May—Marched at five o'clock in the morning, and about one p. m. halted, and pitched our tents for the first time. Prince Cobourg viewed us this day as we passed along, marching by him in slow time.

Head quarters were at a village called Bassing, a fine country all around, with fine crops on the ground.

21st May—Halted to refresh the troops.

22nd May—According to the orders we received, we struck our tents at ten and marched at eleven o'clock a. m., and after a very fatiguing march, on account of the frequent halting of the army, in making the proper disposition for the intended attack next day, we arrived at a fine plain, near which was the Austrian camp of Quiverain: our camp ground was marked out, but we soon received orders to be in readiness to march at 11 o'clock that same night. Having dressed some victuals as time and place would admit, we marched about midnight, with the greatest silence and circumspection, past the Austrian camp towards the enemy.

23rd May—This day the French were forced from their strong camp at Famars, on which occasion the left wing of the allied army, commanded by the Duke of York, eminently distinguished itself. About one o'clock in the morning we halted, and lay upon our arms two hours, giving time for the other parts of the army to make their several movements; a great number of Austrian cavalry and infantry passing by us; we moved forward again about three o'clock, and about four the several dispositions for a general attack being made, it commenced about five, and with such spirit and resolution, on the part of the allied army, that the enemy soon gave way in every quarter, and retreated to Valenciennes.

No general engagement took place, but several partial skirmishes at the detached redoubts of the enemy, which were attacked and defended with much bravery on both sides.

The troops which displayed their valour and activity most, were the Hanoverian flying artillery, with the British light cavalry, and those of the several other nations, as the nature of the engagements were chiefly adapted to their mode of warfare, in pursuing a flying enemy in an open country, where very few impediments occur to obstruct their progress.

It was a glorious fight, as the morning was serene and clear, to see the line of battle formed for an extent of several miles; in one place squadrons of cavalry charging each other in full career, in another the enemy flying and our's pursuing, with the flying artillery, displaying all the skill and dexterity peculiar to themselves; and the brigade of guards was so situated in the morning, that they could behold almost the whole scene of action at one view.

The loss on our side was very small, considering the importance and commanding situation of the hill of Famars, which was also defended with redoubts so advantageously situated, that a determined body of troops might have defended it against a much superior force.

We lay on the ground without our tents this night, which was excessive cold. The foreign troops plundered wherever they came, without hindrance, and generally destroyed what they could not take away: but the British were always strictly forbidden to plunder.

24th May—About three o'clock in the morning we stood to our arms, his Royal Highness the Duke riding along the line, to see the troops get under arms. As we passed Famars, we saw on the top of the hill in the centre of the grand redoubt, the monument created to the memory of the French General Dampier, who was killed by a cannon ball the 8th of May, said to be from the British artillery; his thigh was shot off close to his groin: it was raised ten or twelve feet high, with three sides of painted canvas, with inscriptions in praise of their late commander in chief, and expressive of the prevailing sentiments of that nation; above it arose the common badge of their triumph, the Tree of Liberty, surmounted with the Cap in proper style; it was suffered to remain uninjured by our troops. It is said he was threatened to lose his head if he did not take possession of St. Amand that day on which he was killed.

Valenciennes and Cond, being now left uncovered, the siege of the first was begun in form, and the latter more closely invested.

25th May—A heavy cannonade which commenced yesterday still continued from the outworks of Valenciennes, particularly on the Prussian army, who made near approaches to the north side of the town; in the mean time measures were taken to commence a close siege. His Royal Highness the Duke of York had the chief command of the besieging army, and Prince Cobourg that of the covering army.

A Private of the Coldstream Guards

This is a fine, open, fertile country, delightfully variegated with gentle rising hills, and pleasant valleys; in one of which lies Valenciennes on the river Scheldt. This river washes the north-west part of the town, where there are also some marshy ground, which might retard the approach of an enemy; but the other side, *viz.* the south-east, is a dry, chalky soil, and more level: here the chief, scene of action during the siege was carried on: the trenches extending from near the river side on the east, to Marley, a considerable village, with a fine piece of water on the south: in this village a great number of the enemy made a stand, it being under the cannon of the town.

A considerable quantity of firelocks, pouches, and other warlike instruments, were found in the houses of the country people.

Every house was plundered in a most unfeeling manner, by the Austrians and others of the foreign troops; whose hardened hearts, neither the entreaties of old age, the tears of beauty, the cries of children, nor all the moving scenes of the most accumulated distress, can touch with pity; nor do they content themselves with taking whatever may be useful to them, but destroy whatever they cannot carry away. It would seem the Austrians are not allowed by their laws to plunder in such a degree; for this day one of their officers detected a soldier plundering a poor woman's house of all she had, when, moved with compassion, he ordered him to desist; but he refusing, the officer drew his sword and killed him instantly on the spot.

26th May—Early this morning our troops began a heavy bombardment on the village of Marley, in which a number of French lay; it was soon set on fire, and continued burning the whole day. It could expect no other fate, as it lay between the town and the lines of our encampment.

27th May—Several movements took place in the army, the Austrians taking their post on the right, next the river, the British on the left, and the other auxiliaries between. The head quarters are at Estraux, and the left of the British reaches as far as the heights of Famars. The Prussians, with some other troops, occupies the north side of the river.

28th May—The enemy was very quiet this morning, but in the afternoon several large pieces of ordnance were fired from the town.

30th May—This day a great number of shot and shells were fired from the town.

31st May—The enemy were very quiet during the day, but at night a great number of shot was fired as our piquets advanced pretty near their out-works.

CHAPTER 5

June 1793

1st June—A heavy cannonading was heard towards Conde, which is invested by General Clairfait's army.

2nd June—About ten o'clock at night a working party from the brigade of guards, and the brigade of the line, consisting of about 300 men, and a strong covering party, marched towards the town, and under the direction of the engineer, began the entrenchments; the Austrians at the same time firing according to their strength. The enemy were apprized of it, and fired a great deal; they also threw a number of light balls, with very good judgment; but before three o'clock, each party had made a cover sufficient for their own security.

3rd June—At night, the working parties, etc. as last night. The Prussians amuse them pretty well on the north side of the town as there is often a heavy firing heard on that side.

There are three of our royal family present here at this time, *viz.* his Royal Highness the Duke of York, their Royal Highnesses Prince Ernest Augustus and Prince Adolphus. The weather gets very sultry, but the heaviest part of our duty is always at night. Several skirmishes happen between our advanced piquets and the enemy, who sometimes sally out of their works, but nothing has been done of any consequence.

4th June—We hear that this morning a convoy, consisting of several wagons loaded with provisions and ammunition, are taken from the enemy by our troops. It was designed to be thrown into Valenciennes, but came too late.

The enemy has been very quiet this day; very little firing.

This being his Majesty's birth day, was not observed in any public manner, except in uncasing and displaying our regimental colours.

5th June—The whole of this day a heavy cannonade was heard from Conde. In the evening the enemy attempted to reach our encampments with their shots and shells, but without being able; a shell, however, reached to within a very small distance of the Coldstream quarter guard.

6th June—The enemy have been very quiet this day, hardly a gun has been heard.

7th June—The enemy are very quiet; no cannon has been fired from the town, but they are continually coming out of their batteries at night, firing small shot upon our piquets, which are near them. We have a redoubt with three pieces of cannon mounted on it, which commands the ground near the town, and prevents them from coming much out in the day.

8th June—The enemy very quiet; no firing heard this day.

9th June—Several guns were fired from the town this afternoon, but did no damage. About ten o'clock at night several shells were seen in the air towards Conde.

10th June—Changed our position in the line of encampment this afternoon; during the march of the regiments, the French fired several shots at us, but without effect.

11th June—The enemy were very quiet, very little firing heard during the course of the day.

12th June—A good deal of skirmishing between the advanced piquets this morning, but with little loss on either side.

In the afternoon they fired very heavy on our batteries, and videts; notwithstanding our work goes on briskly, and many batteries, and the entrenchments are in great forwardness. Several of their shot fell very near our videttes; one horse was killed, but the rider was not hurt, and some shot fell not far from our encampment: they continued firing all this afternoon, till darkness put an end to it.

13th June—The enemy fired several pieces of heavy ordnance from the town this morning.

His Royal Highness, the commander in chief, ordered, that a working party, consisting of 750 men, under the command of a field officer, from the brigade of British infantry, should parade this evening on the right of the British encampment: they assembled about half past six o'clock, and marched about eight, with a covering party of 500 men, composed of light dragoons, Austrian heavy cavalry, and Hanoverian grenadiers; they marched towards our works, and immediately began to open the trenches upon the town: the enemy were very quiet during the night.

14th June—This morning they began very early to annoy our men at work, by throwing a great number of shells and shot towards the entrenchments and batteries which we had constructed during the night. A number of their shells burst close to our men, who, though they were very little accustomed to such visitors, soon learned to evade them, by clapping down flat on the ground until they burst.

The working party that went out last night, were relieved this morning about six o'clock, by another of the same strength; they kept working, and the enemy continued firing at small intervals during the course of this day. There were above 4000 men at work, including Austrians, British, Hanoverians, etc.

The enemy threw a vast number of shells in the night at our trenches, which are now in great forwardness; they are wide and deep enough for ammunition wagons to pass and repass unseen by the enemy.

An officer of the Austrians was killed this day by the bursting of a shell in the trenches: an officer of 37th regiment was also wounded by a shell.

None of the British were killed, although several were wounded this day; but a number of the Hanoverian infantry were killed and wounded.

14th June—The enemy continued firing without intermission this day; two men of the 1st regiment of guards were wounded this morning by a shell; also one of the 14th regiment, but not to appearance mortal. Considering the amazing number of shells and shot they threw, and the number of men at work, it is very providential that so few are hurt by them.

During the night, the firing was kept up with the same degree of vigour, but no hurt was sustained on our part during the whole night.

The working parties are relieved twice during the twenty-four hours, namely, in the morning, and evening, and the covering party once, *viz*. in the evening. Duty runs very hard at present with us, having scarcely one night in bed, but the soldiers perform every part of their duty with the utmost cheerfulness.

A surgeon and mate attend constantly in the depots behind the trenches, for the purpose of dressing the wounded men.

His Royal Highness frequently visits the trenches in person, and seems much pleased with the alertness of the men at work.

16th June—This morning an officer of the Austrian engineers was wounded in the head, in two different places, by a shell; a soldier of the light infantry was also wounded in the knee. No material damage was done during the day, and they remained very quiet all the night.

17th June—In the morning commenced a heavy cannonade, which was as briskly answered by an Austrian battery towards the post of Mount Anzin.

About four o'clock in the afternoon the enemy began a terrible cannonade on our trenches, on the left towards the village of Marley, under cover of which some hundreds of them sallied out of the town, on purpose, if possible, to gain possession of our works; but our covering parties repelled them with great spirit, and drove them back to their works, killing and wounding a great number, with very little loss on our side. During the skirmish, one of the 3rd regiment, and one of the 53rd were killed in the trenches by a shell.

18th June—About three o'clock this morning, the enemy began a tremendous fire; about two o'clock p. m. our batteries opened for the first time, and commenced a very warm fire of shot and shells, which soon made them slack their fire. A piece of shell broke the thigh bone of one of the 1st regiment, killed one of the 53rd regiment, and wounded two more.

Our batteries threw into the town, in the course of the night, above 800 shells, which were not answered by the enemy more than one to thirty. Most part of the shot we fired into the town were red a hot, which, with the shells, began to set some parts of it on fire.

19th June—This morning two of our men were killed, one by a grape shot which went through his heart, the other by a cannon ball which went through his body; one belonged to the 1st regiment, the other to the Coldstream grenadiers: they were both on a working party. A surgeon was also wounded in the foot by a Shell.

During the-night, we could see flames burst out in several places of the town, some of which continued burning a long time. When a shell is fired from our batteries, a red hot shot generally accompanies it.

It rained very much all this day, and the enemy kept up but a very slack fire, while dreadful showers of shot and shells poured in upon them from our batteries without intermission.

20th June—The enemy commenced a very brisk fire at daylight, and kept it up till towards the evening, when it began to slacken, but we kept up a constant fire during both day and night. We could perceive great numbers of our shells burst in the town, with a noise resembling distant thunder. It must be very distressing to the inhabitants, for the town is very close built, and the frequent fires seen blazing, is a proof that our artillery does great execution. Five men were wounded in the trenches this day, four of the guards and one of the line.

The enemy fired a great deal from their outworks, with small arms, this evening, but did us no damage.

21st June—This morning we could plainly perceive a breach made in the side of the steeple of the great church. During this day the enemy were much more quiet than they have been since the trenches have been opened.

About eleven o'clock at night, some new mortar batteries opened upon the enemy, and threw a vast number of shells into the town, accompanied, as usual, with red hot shot.

22nd June—Between twelve and one o'clock this morning we perceived the large buildings on the left of the great church to be on fire; it continued burning with great fury till it was consumed to the ground, the fire of which communicating with the main body of the church, set it all on a blaze: this church was one of their principal magazines, for forage, arms, etc. about four o'clock the roof fell in, when the flames burst out with greater fury than ever.

Two other fires raged with uncontrollable fury in the town at the same time, but we could not see the effects of them, as the works of the town intercepted our fight.

While that raging element, fire, was destroying all before it, in several places with irresistible force, and flaming showers of shells and shot descending in all parts of the town, the darkness of the night made more dreadful by sudden death glaring in all his fiery terrors, added to the tremendous thunder of artillery all around, mixed with groans and loud cries of wounded and dying men, women, and children!

The anguish and distress of the wretched inhabitants may, in part, be conceived, but can never be described by human tongue or pen. By the light of the fire we could plainly perceive the French running to and fro in great confusion, and at some intervals could hear their clamorous noise. They fired but very little during the night, but all our batteries played on the town without intermission.

This morning a shell burst close to a Hanoverian soldier, as he was asleep in the trenches; his body was blown all to atoms, and never seen more, except one arm, which was found in the trench.

Our approaches are carrying on very close to the town, our men can hear them talking very plain in their works.

They are continually firing musketry at our working men, endeavouring to hit their heads as they throw the earth over the trench.

This afternoon two deserters came in to us from the enemy, who fired several shot after them, but without effect; they say the French are in great want, both of provisions and ammunition, and that the inhabitants would fain prevail upon the governor to give up the town before it is quite destroyed.

The enemy have been very quiet during the whole day, and at night our batteries began with redoubled fury again, and set the town on fire in four places; eight or ten shells might be seen blazing above the town at one time. The fire lasted for several hours, and burnt with great fury.

23rd June—The enemy have been remarkably quiet this day, as well as yesterday, the reason of which we cannot conjecture; but our batteries keep firing with unremitting activity, especially in the night time, which never fail setting some part of the town on fire.

Another deserter came in from the enemy this afternoon, with his arms and accoutrements; he says, a vast number of the people in the town are killed and wounded, and many hundreds of houses burnt down, and that many of his comrades would willingly come over to us, if they could find opportunity.

24th June—The enemy kept up a kind of faint fire this day. A 3rd regiment grenadier got up to look over the trench towards the enemy, and turning to speak to some one behind him, a cannon ball took his head clean off: another of the 3rd regiment was wounded by a shell. The firing from our batteries continues with the same activity.

25th June—This morning some new batteries were opened on the town, from a height which lies a considerable way to the left of our lines; they were all manned with British artillery, and constructed under the direction of Major Wright of our artillery, who commanded them. As they lay on a commanding eminence, they annoy the enemy very much, who returned their fire very briskly.

26th June—As our new batteries direct their shot and shells with great judgment, which distress the enemy very much, they returned their fire this day with great fury; but during the night they fired very little, while all the batteries round the town kept thundering away without intermission.

The weather has been remarkably wet ever since the trenches were opened, which is a very disagreeable circumstance.

27th June—The enemy direct their attention chiefly to our new batteries, which gall them very much.

This evening, for a little time, not a gun was fired from either side, but at night our batteries re-commenced firing again with their usual ardour.

28th June—The firing from our lines kept up with the usual vigour; the enemy fired very little towards the lines, but the new batteries seem to take all their attention, a proof that they suffer a great deal by them.

29th June—Very early this morning our batteries from the lines opened the warmest fire upon the enemy's works that has been since the siege began; it forced them to abandon their horn-works, and did them considerable damage.

Yesterday afternoon three of the towns people made their escape into the trenches; they had been sent out to cut forage, and no guard being with them, as was customary, they took that opportunity to make off. Being conducted to head quarters, his Royal Highness examined them himself; they said that the greatest part of the inhabitants of the town wished to give it up, but the general and the artillery were determined to hold it out to the last extremity.

This morning three more of the inhabitants made their escape. At night our batteries continued firing as usual.

30th June—Three of the guards were wounded this day, one mortally, belonging to the 1st regiment. The firing continued as usual.

CHAPTER 6

July 1793

1st July—The firing continued with great fury from our batteries, as on the preceding day.

The left of our trenches reached as far as the village of Marley, which was burnt down on the 26th of May last, and the first battery on the left consisted of four long eighteen pounders: next to that was a battery mounting six thirteen and one-half inch mortars: next was one of four long eighteen pounders: then another of six long eighteen pounders: next another of six thirteen and one-half inch mortars: next to that one of ten and one-half inch howitzers: next, a fine battery of six twenty-four pounders: there are several batteries besides these in the rear on the heights.

2nd July—The firing continued from our lines as usual into their out-works, which harassed them not a little, as we could perceive them at work all day; they threw several howitzer shells into our advanced parallels, but did very little damage, besides wounding one man of the working party.

Several of their shells fell near our trenches and did not burn: at all, which must be owing to some defect in the fusee.

Our batteries threw a vast number of shells into the town during the night, which were faintly answered by the enemy.

3rd July—This day Lieutenant-Colonel the Earl of Cavan was wounded in the head by a piece of a shell; it is thought not to be dangerous. The night passed as usual.

4th July—This day our batteries kept up a brisk fire on the town, and all the night our riflemen on the advanced posts kept up a constant fire of small arms upon those of the enemy. Five men belonging to the guards were wounded this day.

5th July—We kept working, and the enemy continued firing howitzer shells into our second parallel; they threw several shells directly into the trench, but luckily only one man was killed; he belonged to the 14th foot, a shell fell on him as he stood in the trench, and severed his body in two.

Our trenches are carried very near the enemy's works, and our men are constantly railing at the French over the trenches; we can see the effects of our shot in some of their large buildings, which appear full of holes like a sieve.

6th July—A shell from the enemy this forenoon fell into a small magazine of powder, behind one of the batteries, which it blew up, with an Austrian officer of artillery, and a corporal; some small fragments of their bodies and clothes were found afterwards: one of the 3rd regiment was killed, and one of the 1st regiment wounded.

Yesterday afternoon an Irishman, belonging to the 14th regiment of foot, deserted to the enemy; he got over unperceived by any of our men, but as he was climbing over the enemy's palisades, an Austrian rifleman observed him, and immediately acquainted our officers. During the night our batteries kept up a heavy fire on the town, and set several parts of it on fire, which burned all night.

The enemy still continue a heavy cannonade on Major Wright's battery; one of the guns was dismounted yesterday, two men killed, and several wounded.

7th July—This morning a shell fell into our trench, it burst, and wounded five men of the 53rd regiment, some very dangerously.

The enemy did not fire much this forenoon, but at night as usual.

8th July—The enemy has brought a number of guns and mortars to an angle of their works, from which they have played pretty smartly this day, but have not done us much damage.

An accident happened to a soldier of the 16th regiment of light dragoons this day, he had got a shell into the camp by some means or other, and curiosity excited him to try to get the fusee out, in doing of which it caught fire between his legs, and tore one thigh and the other leg entirely off; he died soon after.

In the evening one of the 1st regiment was wounded in the arm so badly, that it was cut off as soon as he reached the hospital.

9th July—Early this morning a soldier of the Coldstream was killed by a shell in the trenches, and in the afternoon another belonging to the 3rd regiment was wounded. About 10 o'clock at night our mortar batteries began a tremendous fire upon the town, and in a short time a great fire broke out, seemingly about the centre of the town, which raged with great fury, and spread a considerable way all round.

10th July—Our batteries kept roaring continually upon the enemy, which was but faintly answered by them. This morning a sergeant of the 14th regiment had a piece of his thigh taken away by a shell as he was coming out of the trenches.

In the forenoon our shells set the town on fire in two places, which burnt more fiercely than any fire which has happened in the day time; the flames, though the sun was shining very bright, were plain to be seen burning out from behind a large building covered with slate.

This evening we received the agreeable intelligence that Conde has surrendered to the Imperial arms; this will greatly facilitate our operations against Valenciennes.

At night the enemy threw shells and hand grenades towards our trenches for the first time, but our batteries in return sent shells, hand grenades, and baskets filled with flint stones, which were fired out of mortars directly into their works; no damage was sustained on our side during the night.

11th July—This morning another large fire was kindled in their works, which burnt till about six o'clock, when they got it under control by some means or other. One man of the 1st regiment of grenadiers was wounded this day.

A great number of miners have been employed some time in carrying several mines from the trenches towards the town.

The weather is excessive hot at present.

Our artillery kept thundering at the town all night as usual, which was faintly returned by the enemy.

12th July—This day one of the Coldstream regiment was dangerously wounded by a piece of a shell which took his foot off; the firing kept up at night as usual.

13th July—This day the French troops marched out of Conde, and some distance from the town, laid down their arms, and surrendered themselves to the Austrian troops.

During this day and night our batteries kept firing with great fury as usual.

14th July—This morning all the troops around Valenciennes fired a *feu-de-joie* for the taking of Conde; also our batteries redoubled their fire at the same time against the town, and at night as usual.

15th July—This day a soldier of the 1st regiment was dangerously wounded with a shell. Heavy firing at night as usual.

16th July—This morning about five o'clock a trumpet was sounded from the enemy's works, as a signal for a parley; in consequence of which the firing ceased on both sides immediately; a flag of truce came out to our trenches, and was conducted to his Royal Highness the Duke of York.

During the interval of firing, our men went out of the trenches towards them, and conversed with each other a considerable time, with all the familiarity and good nature imaginable; they seemed willing to give the town up, only they say their Governor, General Ferrand, dares not do it, until he has defended it a certain time.

The purport of the flag of truce was, to demand leave for a lady, near the time of her delivery, to leave the town, which his Royal Highness accordingly granted.

About eleven o'clock this forenoon, at which time the truce expired, a gun was fired from the town, as a signal for each party to prepare for action; it was laughable to see our men (who till that moment stood talking with the French) running to their posts, and tumbling neck and heels into their trenches. The firing then commenced on both sides with redoubled vigour, and continued all the afternoon; and our people at night as usual.

Our third parallel is now completed, the batteries finished, and the guns mounted. This parallel is carried very close to the enemy's lines, and when the batteries open, must, of course, do great execution. Our mines are also ready for springing, the powder has been conveyed into the chambers some nights since. Our working parties are discontinued, and every thing being thus finished and ready, Should the garrison hold out much longer after the opening of the third parallel, it is thought the town will be stormed.

17th July—The firing continued this day and night as usual. One of the 3rd regiment was wounded by a shell as the covering party entered the trenches.

18th July—This day four of the Coldstream were wounded by a shell, one very dangerously, having his arm taken off during the night. Firing as usual.

19th July—A sergeant of 14th regiment was killed, and two soldiers of the same regiment wounded. At night the enemy threw a number of shells towards our trenches, but did no damage.

20th July—This day two of our light infantry were wounded by a shell. At night the enemy fired a great deal of musketry from their horn-works, but with very little effect.

21st July—The weather is fine and dry, which makes our duty much more agreeable. Firing as usual.

22nd July—A grenadier of the 1st regiment was killed by a shell this day. The firing kept up with as much spirit as usual.

23rd July—This morning at four o'clock, several new batteries on the third parallel opened upon the town with much spirit, that in a few hours they silenced many of the enemy's guns; and at night continued with redoubled fury. One man of the 3rd regiment was killed, and two wounded, one of which had both his legs and arms taken off.

24th July—A very heavy fire, both of shells and shot this day; only one of the 1st regiment of grenadiers was wounded, but a great number of the Hanoverian and Austrian artillery were killed and wounded. Our British artillery manned some of the new batteries which were opened yesterday morning, two were killed, and one lost his leg yesterday, and one was blown up by an accident of some powder catching fire.

The enemy's fire since the opening of these last mentioned batteries, has been very languid. A great deal of musketry fired during the night.

25th July—This afternoon a number of men was ordered for the purpose of storming the out-works of the town this evening. The British infantry furnished 300 men, *viz*. 150 from the brigade of guards, and 150 from the brigade of the line, under the command of Major-General Abercrombie. We were ordered to be in readiness at the centre communication, at Marley, in the evening. It was pre-concerted to spring three mines, and immediately after the springing of the last, the troops were to begin the attack.

Accordingly in the evening the first mine was sprung, then the second, and third, with the space of eight minutes between each. Immediately on the springing of the third, the troops being ready, rushed in with the utmost impetuosity, jumping over the palisadoes, and through the breaches the mines had made, like the rushing of a flood, and carried all before them at the point of the bayonet. The enemy made a stout resistance, but were forced to leave us in possession of their works.

There was a great number killed on both sides, but the brigade of guards suffered but little; yet we have to regret the loss of Capt. Tollemache, killed, and Captain Warde of the same regiment wounded. An officer of the 14th regiment was killed.

The 1st regiment had one rank and file killed, one sergeant, and three rank and file wounded. Coldstream, two rank and file wounded. Third regiment, one sergeant, and one rank and file wounded.

His Royal Highness expressed the greatest satisfaction with the conduct of the officers and men employed on this expedition.

26th July—This day the enemy fired very little; we suppose last night's work has somewhat humbled their pride. We had a grenadier of the 1st regiment killed this day, and three of the 3rd wounded, one of which died next day. The 1st regiment had one wounded.

Very late this night a flag of truce was sent in to the governor, with a summons to surrender, or otherwise threatening to storm the town. The firing immediately ceased on both sides.

27th July—Not a gun had been fired on either side this day; it is said the governor has a certain time allowed to consider of his final answer.

Nine deserters came over to us this day, and an officer, who says the enemy are beginning to disagree among themselves, so that of course they must soon surrender. One of the deserters who speaks a little English, says, that on our storming their out-works, they were thrown into the greatest confusion imaginable. No firing this night.

28th July—This morning about' six o'clock, a flag of truce was sent from head quarters to require General Ferrand's final answer; but before they reached the town, they met a general of the French, accompanied by three officers, a sergeant, and a trumpeter, who were sent from the town to settle the terms of the capitulation.

Accordingly the terms were agreed upon, and this evening a detachment from the British infantry, consisting of 400 men, under the command of Colonel Sir James Duff, took possession of the outer gate of Valenciennes, leading to Cambray.

All quiet this night.

29th July—On the 27th a draught from England joined the brigade of guards, under the command of Colonel Watson of the 3rd regiment, consisting of near 600 men, among them were three light infantry companies, one from each regiment, *viz.* the 1st company commanded by Lieutenant-Colonel Ludlow; Coldstream by Lieutenant-Colonel Eld; and the 3rd regiment by Lieutenant-Colonel Campbell, which three companies were joined to the flank battalion of guards, which now consisted of eight companies.

30th July—This morning the Hanoverian grenadiers relieved the British detachment at the town-gate.

31st July—The troops are cleaning themselves, and preparing to take possession of the town to-morrow, which is the day appointed for the French marching out of it.

Chapter 7

August 1793

1st August—This morning the French troops marched out of the town with all the honours of war, drums beating, colours flying, and a few field pieces, and all their baggage, etc. and after getting to a convenient place, they laid down their arms, and marched off to their own country.

The garrison consisted still of about 7000 effective men. From the hardness of their duty, in the obstinate defence they made, it could not be expected for them to make a fine appearance; notwithstanding some squadrons of their cavalry looked exceeding well, their clothing uniform, and their horses in good condition, but a great number of the infantry were of a very small stature, and their clothing in general very ragged.

They had a number of fine women, clean, and well dressed, riding on their baggage wagons.

The army formed two lines, one on each side of the road leading to Cambray, to a vast extent, between which they marched along; some looked very cheerful, others fierce and disdainful. General Ferrand, who rode at the head of the line, had a very solemn countenance, rather downcast.

Prince Cobourg and the Duke of York, were both present; the former had an exceeding numerous train of attendants.

The men who were employed on the storming party on the 25th of July, were all posted next the Cambray gate, whilst the French troops marched out, as a post of honour.

After the troops were clear out of the town, the magistrates came and delivered the keys to Prince Cobourg and the Duke of York, in the usual formality. A garrison of the Austrian troops then took possession of it.

2nd August—The British and other troops had leave given them to view the town of Valenciennes.

To view it from the ramparts on the east side of the town, which was most exposed to our cannon, nothing could appear more distressed and ruinous; not a house could be seen that was not either burnt or partly thrown down; the streets filled with rubbish, mixed with cannon balls and pieces of shells. The miserable inhabitants who now durst crawl out of their hiding places, looked blank and doubtful; they were released from the terrors of death, but their all was destroyed, and the uncertainty of their future condition impressed the marks of dejection deeply on every countenance.

3rd August—We viewed some of the hospitals in the town, they were all crowded with sick or wounded men, women and children of all ages: in one of them, five carcases lay in a corner, piled one upon another; and in another place was a child lying unburied, and others dying every hour. We are informed there were 13,000 troops in the town at the beginning of the siege, and only 7000 marched out; the rest are either dead or in the hospitals.

4th August—Provisions of every kind are crowding into the town, and it begins to assume a more cheerful aspect.

The Emperor is going to repair the town and fortifications as soon as possible.

5th August—This day the man who deserted from the 14th regiment of foot, on the 5th of July (having been found in the town when it was delivered up, and tried by a general court martial) was hung on a tree behind the British encampment. Orders issued to march to-morrow morning at five o'clock. The French having a considerable force in or near Cambray, the movement is intended against them.

6th August—This morning the heavy baggage was sent off to St. Amand, and twelve tents per company ordered to go with us. About six o'clock we marched, and after a fatiguing journey, on account of the excessive heat of the weather, we arrived at a piece of ground about fourteen miles distant, where we pitched our camp, except the flank battalion, which, as an advanced piquet, lodged in a village about a mile distant.

7th August—The army marched about three o'clock this morning, in a direction towards the south of Cambray.

As it was a fine open country, we were under no necessity of keeping to the roads, but made our own roads according to the intended route, almost like a ship at sea.

This afternoon, about the time we halted, the 15th regiment of light dragoons, being on the advanced guard, fell in with upwards of 200 of the enemy's cavalry, which they completely routed, killed several, and took prisoners, two officers, and forty-four men, with sixteen led horses.

8th August—This morning at four o'clock the army was in motion, and the French having retreated, we made a circuit round the south side of Cambray; being within view of that famous town, and encamped near the village of Bourlon, in which village the flank battalion was quartered.

9th August—The army halted this day to refresh the troops. The village of Bourlon lies to the west of Cambray, about six miles distant; it is a delightful country, the prospect being continually diversified, with gentle rising hills, fruitful villages, and fine crops on the ground.

10th August—About eight o'clock this morning the army marched, fetching our circuit round the north side of Cambray, and directing our course eastward, we passed several redoubts, entrenchments, etc. of the enemy, this day, some constructed with much art and labour. We now bent our course towards Marchiennes, and pitched near the village of Bruille.

11th August—About seven o'clock this morning the army was in motion, and passing through the town of Marchiennes, marched along the *chaussee* to Orchies, near which place the army encamped.

12th August—The army halted, and the heavy baggage which was sent from Valenciennes to St. Amand, joined us.

14th August—The siege of Dunkirk being determined upon, under the command of his Royal Highness the Duke of York, and the covering army under the command of General Freytag, part of our army marched this day on their route for that place.

15th August—Struck our tents and marched at five o'clock this morning, passed Tournay on our right, and encamped seven or eight miles west of that place, near a small village called Rue.

16th August—Marched about four o'clock in the morning; passed through Lannoy (in which were some Prussian cavalry) leaving Doubaix on our left, and through Tourcoign, near which place we encamped. The Dutch troops occupy Tourcoign.

We lay this night, as we have several nights before, without our tents, the baggage not coming up.

The Austrian light cavalry which covered our left flank towards Lille, this day had several slight skirmishes with the French.

17th August—The brigade of guards halted this day, except the flank battalion, which marched in the morning, passed though Menin, and encamped near a village called Ghelius, with some other corps. A remarkable shower of rain fell this day, after these troops had passed through Menin.

18th August—The flank battalion halted, and the other three battalions marching in the morning, halted near Menin on their arms.

The Dutch troops having been driven from the port of Lincelles this day, it was deemed necessary to retake it; upon which the three battalions of the guards, under the command of Major-General Lake, were ordered immediately on that service; accordingly we marched about two o'clock p. m. and about six o'clock reached the village of Lincelles, where we found the enemy strongly entrenched, and well prepared for their defence.

General Lake having made the proper disposition, the attack began. The 1st regiment being in front of the column, began the attack, and the 3rd regiment and Coldstream forming on their left with the utmost celerity, the whole line then rushed in upon the enemy with irresistible force, amidst showers of grape shot from their redoubts; and after discharging a volley or two of musketry, made a furious charge, accompanied with a loud *huzza*, mounted their batteries in the face of the enemy, and devoted all they met with to the bayonet.

The French, who had been accustomed to the cold lifeless attacks of the Dutch, were amazed at the spirit and intrepidity of the British, and not much relishing the manner of our salute, immediately gave way, abandoning all that was in the place, and in their flight threw away both arms and accoutrements.

We took one stand of colours, ten pieces of cannon, with two pieces which they had taken from the Dutch, and a number of prisoners. We suppose the number of troops in that place to have amounted to between 5 and 6000; ours were short of 1200.

The following is a return of our loss, in killed and wounded.

	Capt.		Lieut.		Ensn		Sergt.		Drum.		R & F	
	Killed	Wounded	Killed	Wounded	Killed	Wounded	Killed	Wounded	Killed	Wounded	Killed	Wounded
1st Regiment		2		3			2	2			19	42
Coldstream	1	1				1		2			8	40
3rd Regiment				1				2	1		7	43
Total	1	3		4		1	2	6	1		34	125

Lieutenant-Colonel Bosville of the Coldstream was killed, a man of an amiable disposition, much regretted by all who knew him.

About ten o'clock at night our troops having left off the pursuit, all was quiet; and the 53rd. and 14th regiments, with some Hessian infantry, coming to relieve us, we marched back to our former ground near Menin, which we reached about three o'clock in the morning, much fatigued.

19th August—The troops halted this day, and the late Lieutenant-Colonel Bosville was buried; and also Lieutenant Depoister of the royal artillery, attached to the 3rd regiment, who was killed yesterday.

20th August—Marched about five o'clock this morning, and in our route passed through the small, but strong town of Ypres, and encamped near a small village called Boesinghe. The brigade of guards lay in an orchard very pleasantly situated.

21st August—At four in the morning the army was in motion, and in our route passed through Furnes, near which town we encamped.

22nd August—About four o'clock in the afternoon we marched towards Dunkirk: at the same time the French camp at Gyvelde, which covered Dunkirk, was attacked, and forced; as also several batteries they had created in the road by the side of the canal, from thence to Dunkirk.

We lay upon our arms among the sand hills, near Gyvelde, all night, which was excessive cold. Some of the soldiers observing a barn not far off, soon dislodged some of the straw, wheat, barley, etc. that was in it, to cover themselves with.

23rd August—As soon as it was light, we marched towards Dunkirk in several columns; the guards marched through the village of Gyvelde, where the French camp had been, and along the dyke on the side of the Furnes canal; the Austrians on the right toward the sea; the Hanoverians, Hessians, etc. on the left towards Fort Louis, etc. which fort, after a severe engagement, the Hanoverians took possession of.

The Austrians began cannonading some batteries the French had erected on the sand-hills, to oppose them, and drove them back near the town. Our column met with no opposition this day, but marched quietly along the side of the canal, to within about two miles and a half, or three miles of Dunkirk. The three battalions of the guards encamped about a mile to the left of the canal, and the flank battalion encamped in a large field on the right, along with the brigade of the line, etc.

The country people almost all left their houses to the mercy of the army, who made free with what provisions they could find, such as bread, pigs, poultry, etc. As we came up the side of the canal, we saw dead men and horses, which had been killed in the action the night before. There is a very high tower on Dunkirk, from the top of which they can see all the country round, and which will perhaps prove prejudicial to us, as from thence they may observe all our movements.

24th August—A general attack was made on the enemy's out-posts. The flank battalion advanced through a large track of garden ground, and other enclosures, surrounded with deep ditches full of water, and strong double hedges, through which they forced their way with their usual intrepidity, obliging the enemy to retreat back to the town with precipitation. We suffered very little from their musketry, because they never attempted to dispute the ground with us, but kept firing and retreating; but they were no sooner got under cover of their own guns, than they began to open upon us with both grape and round shot; and although the hedges, etc. covered us pretty well from their fight, they could not defend us from their shot, and in our retreat to a convenient cover, we suffered considerably, both in killed and wounded. The three battalions did not advance., but stood in readiness at a convenient distance.

The two guns attached to the flank battalion did infinite execution, among the French infantry as they retreated, having got the command of a certain spot over which the enemy must pass, they cut them down by platoons at a time; but they suffered severely for their bravery; two pieces of cannon which the French had brought to bear upon them, played with unremitting activity, and before night there were but two artillery men of both the guns that was not either killed or wounded.

Among the slain this day was Lieutenant-Colonel Eld, captain of the Coldstream light company, of whom he was remarkably fond, but had never seen their courage tried till this day, and while in the act of encouraging and praising them for their cool and steady valour, was shot through the heart with a cannon ball. Thus fell a brave and experienced officer, lamented by all who knew him.

Lieutenant-General Dalton, a brave officer in the Austrian service, was also killed, and Captain Williams of the flank battalion was wounded, and about forty rank and file killed and wounded.

25th August—The siege of Dunkirk cannot be carried on by trenches, etc. as that of Valenciennes, on account of the lowness of the ground, intersected with deep ditches, which they can inundate at pleasure, therefore a chain of redoubts is begun, constructed with gabions, fascines, etc. with communications between.

26th August—The flank battalion changed its position, and encamped near the rest of the brigade; several other changes of situation took place in the line.

27th August—A great deal of heavy artillery is arrived from Ostend by the canal. The enemy remain very quiet, and our work goes on with the greatest activity.

28th August—Ten twenty-four pounders were landed this day, with shot, shells, etc. Numerous detachments at work in every quarter, making fascines, gabions, etc.

The British shipping which were expected here as soon as the army, is not yet in sight, while the enemy have two frigates and other vessels cruising about the mouth of the port.

CHAPTER 8

September 1793

6th September—The enemy made a desperate sortie this afternoon, chiefly on our right flank towards the sea. The Austrians, with our brigade of the line, artillery, etc. stood a most severe conflict, and at last obliged them to retire with great loss. Our loss was also very considerable, and unfortunately among the killed was that brave officer and able engineer, Colonel Moncrief,

7th September—The continual rainy weather, and the inundation together, has filled all the ditches and other low places with water, so that we can hardly pass from one place to another without swimming; a great deal of the camp ground was also overflowed,

8th September—General Freytag, whose corps covers the siege of this place, was attacked yesterday, and to-day, with a force so superior, as to be obliged to retreat to Hondschoote, which necessarily constrained his Royal Highness the Duke of York to raise the siege with precipitation.

Accordingly about eleven o'clock at night, having struck our tents, loaded the baggage, etc. we began our march, sending off the baggage first, but for want of horses, and the shortness of the time, were obliged to leave about thirty pieces of heavy artillery behind. We marched all night, and in the morning arrived at Furnes, and halted on the ground we formerly occupied; but a great deal of our baggage was lost, owing to the darkness of the night, and the heavy sandy roads through which it had to pass.

9th September—Halted on our former ground without tents, our baggage not being unloaded.

10th September—The flank battalion, with some light cavalry, moved off this evening, and after marching some miles towards Loo, halted a few hours, and then returned back near Furnes, where we found some of the other battalions also in motion; we formed together in a field east of the town, in a kind of irregular column, there we rested till day-light next morning.

11th September—Crossed a few fields eastward, and halted this day, but no tents, the baggage being sent off towards Ostend.

12th September—Marched about three o'clock this morning, taking our route by Aven Capelle, to Dixmuyde, near which town we halted.

13th September—Halted this day to rest the troops; the baggage arrived from Ostend, but we did not pitch our tents.

14th September—Marched about two in the morning; on our route the 19th, 57th, and three companies of the 42nd regiment joined us, having landed at Ostend that morning; we halted that night, (for it was night before we reached the place,) along the side of the high road, near Thorout; dressed some victuals, chiefly potatoes, as many of us lay among them, and betook ourselves to rest without our tents.

15th September—About five o'clock this morning we were under arms, and marched towards Roufelaire, a handsome town on the Mundel river, we passed through it, and halted about two miles southwards towards Menin; it rained very much this night.

16th September—At three o'clock this afternoon we arrived near Menin, and pitched our camp on the same ground we occupied before, on the 18th of August.

Menin is a very unfortunate town, the Dutch troops being left to defend it, on our going to Dunkirk, the French drove them out, and plundered the town; they had formed a camp outside the town, but retreated on our approach.

17th September—Remained in camp, the weather very wet.

23rd September—Changed the position of our camp, about a mile farther back, in order to take the advantage of a piece of dry ground, which is a very good situation; a small brook runs along the front of the camp, which makes it both pleasant and convenient.

24th September—The enemy are in considerable force about Werwick, Commines, etc. and our out-posts extend to Hallian, Albeke, etc.: several skirmishes take place, but none as yet of any consequence.

25th September—The 1st battalion 1st regiment having lost all their tents in the retreat from Dunkirk, are now cantoned in a small village behind Menin.

26th September—On account of the cold and wetness of the weather, his Royal Highness has been pleased to order a quantity of rum to be given every day to each man.

We also have begun to thatch our tents, or rather to make

huts; which defend us much better from the cold. This camp is better supplied with every necessary article, such as butter, cheese, milk, etc. than any we have yet seen, and at very reasonable prices.

Chapter 9

October 1793

10th October—The brigade of guards, with several other corps, marched at five o'clock this morning, and passing through Menin and Courtray arrived at Peck, a village on the Courtray road, about seven miles from Tournay, where we were quartered, and in the adjacent places.

11th October—Marched about five o'clock in the morning, and encamped in the afternoon on the plain of Cysoign, near Camphin.

12th October—Halted.

13th October—Halted.

14th October—Marched about two o'clock in the afternoon, and after a very fatiguing journey reached St. Amand about ten at night. Lay in the old monastery.

15th October—About seven in the morning we left St. Amand, and in our route passed close under the walls of Valenciennes; the trenches are all filled up, and the works of the town much repaired.
Encamped on the heights near the village of Soultain.

16th October—Marched at eight o'clock this morning, and passed close under the walls of Quefnoy, which surrendered to General Clairfait on the 11th of September last, after a short siege; it is a handsome compact town, well fortified, and stands on a commanding eminence, with a fine open country around it.

We encamped this evening at Englefontaine, about half way between Quefnoy and Landrecy. Our brigade occupied some huts which had been created by some part of our army, who were now removed to another quarter.

This day and yesterday the French made a violent attack on General Clairfait, who covered the siege of Maubeuge. On the former day they were defeated, but on the second they succeeded in cutting off his communication with the besieging army, which obliged the Prince of Cobourg to relinquish his undertaking.

It is, however, a singular circumstance, that notwithstanding the issue proved unfavourable, twenty-two pieces of cannon and two howitzers were taken by the Austrians in those two days without any being lost by them.

This circumstance, perhaps, made it unnecessary for us to proceed any further on our present route.

17th October—Halted at Englefontaine.

19th October—Received the news in our camp that the Prussians under General Warmer had forced the strong lines of Weissembourg, and obtained a most complete victory over the French.

20th October—This day, in consequence of the above victory, the British troops fired a *feu-de-joie*.

Our troops are formed under arms an hour before day break every morning, in readiness, if the enemy should make an attack.

23rd October—Received orders this morning to be in readiness to march at two o'clock p. m. accordingly about three, we marched back the same road we came, passing Quefnoy, and encamped in the plain near Valenciennes; it froze hard, and the cold this night was excessive severe.

24th October—At four o'clock this morning we were under arms, and again passed under the walls of Valenciennes, but were not suffered to march through the town. All hands are employed in repairing the works, and the inhabitants have begun to rebuild the desolated village of Marlis, which was burnt at the commencement of the siege on the 26th of June last.

We repassed through St. Amand, and encamped on the hill of Maulde.

25th October—About three in the morning we marched from the camp at Maulde, towards Tournay, and leaving it on our right, encamped about three miles distant, on the Orchies road.

26th October—Halted there; wet stormy weather.

27th October—Removed, and pitched our camp near our former ground, on the plains of Cysoign.

28th October—About eleven o'clock, the flank battalion and 3rd regiment of guards, with some squadrons of the 15th light dragoons, two howitzers, and four field pieces, were ordered to march immediately, in order to attack the enemy, who were strongly posted in the village of Lannoy, about six miles from our camp: about twelve o'clock we marched, and on arriving there, the artillery advanced, covered by the infantry, and commenced a brisk cannonade on the enemy, which continued upwards of two hours, and was answered by the French; but finding it too hot for them, they abandoned the village, which General Abercrombie, who commanded, perceiving, ordered the light cavalry to pursue them, which they did, with a spirit and activity peculiar to themselves; killed about fifty, and brought back near 100 prisoners, among whom were several officers.

Captain Sutherland, of the royal military artificers, riding across an avenue, where some guns of the enemy pointed, received a mortal wound by a cannon ball in the thigh, of which he died in a few minutes after. Captain Thornton of the royal artillery, attached to the flank battalion, received a wound by which he lost his arm. Lieutenant Rutherford of the artificers received a wound from the enemy, and then was cut in the head by one of our own dragoons, mistaking him for a French officer, he having a great coat over his regimentals; two of the 3rd regiment were wounded, one of which soon died; two or three of the light cavalry were killed or wounded.

By the report of the prisoners, there were about 1600 hundred in the village when the action began. About one o'clock next morning we returned home to our camp.

One of the Austrian battalions of Starry supported our left flank; and though all the troops behaved with the greatest bravery, yet the artillery deserve to be particularly distinguished, for they worked their guns with amazing activity and judgment, and although not half the number, proved an overmatch for the French, who, notwithstanding, are in general good artillery-men.

30th October—This day the town of Marchiennes was surprised and taken by a party of the Austrians, and the whole of the troops that were there, taken prisoners; they consisted of about 300 cavalry, and 1200 infantry, and were brought here to head quarters .

31st October—A number of prisoners were brought in this day also from the advanced posts.

CHAPTER 10
November 1793

3rd November—Seldom a day passes but some prisoners are brought in from one quarter or another.

The weather continues to be very wet and cold, and the ground we lie upon is very soft and dirty, in consequence of which his Royal Highness has ordered an additional quantity of wood. to be issued out to the men; and also a quantity of liquor, which not a little contributes to preserve the health and spirits of the troops,

9th November—At nine o'clock this morning we struck our tents once more, being the twenty-fourth and last time this campaign, and marched into Tournay, and were conducted to that extensive range of barracks, on the north side of the river, which we found much more comfortable than our late situation.

Thus our brigade ended a campaign in which we have constantly (except at Dunkirk) been crowned with success; and the failure in that one instance was most evidently neither owing to want of courage in the troops engaged in it, nor ability in our royal commander, but to a combination of events and disappointments which it is not my province to investigate.

All the army are not restored to quarters, but are chiefly cantoned along the frontier, where they can most conveniently watch the enemy's motions.

24th November—Nothing material occurred with us, until the 24th instant, when all the troops here assembled on the esplanade, and fired a *feu-de-joie* on the news of Fort Louis, on the Rhine, having surrendered to General Wurmser on the 14th instant. In it 4000 men, and 112 pieces of ordnance were taken, with a very large quantity of stores, etc.

CHAPTER 11

December 1793

11th December—Nothing worth notice has happened, except the frequent arrival of French prisoners from the out-posts.

The brigade of guards, with several regiments of heavy cavalry, are ordered to Ghent for the winter. The brigade of the line, and light cavalry, with several other corps, remain under the command of General Abercrombie, on the out-posts.

14th December—This morning at eight o'clock the brigade of guards, with some regiments of cavalry, marched from Tournay, and were quartered this night at a number of small villages, *viz.* Avelghom, Hestert, Waermaerde, etc. we were ordered to march at seven o'clock next morning.

15th December—Marched at seven o'clock, and in our route passed close by Oudenarde, and were quartered as last night at Heurne, Ouweghem, etc.

16th December—Marched at eight in the morning, and arrived at Ghent about two o'clock, p. m. and were conducted to the different barracks provided for us, *viz.* the Coldstream and 3rd regiment battalions to St. Peter's barracks, near St. Peter's church; the flank battalion and 1st regiment to temporary barracks, created in a large building, formerly a nunnery, situated near the side of the Bruges canal.

The duty here is regular, and furnished by the four battalions of guards in rotation. Two battalions are under arms on the grand place every morning, *viz.* the battalion that furnishes the guards, and the next in rotation, which falls in behind the former in readiness.

The town-major makes up the different guards, and regulates the duty; after which the field officer for the day marches off the guards, who, with the battalion in waiting, marches by divisions and open ranks past the commander in chief, preceded by three piquets of cavalry, which relieve daily.

CHAPTER 12

January 1794

18th January—This day the troops here, consisting of 18th. cavalry, infantry, and the artillery attached to them, were drawn up on the banks of the canal leading to Bruges, and fired a *feu-de-joie* in honour of her Majesty's birth day. The artillery fired a royal salute of twenty-four guns; the cavalry discharged their pistols, and the whole exhibited a very fine appearance.

His Royal Highness invited the officers and gentry of the town to an entertainment in the evening.

24th January—The frost sets in very severe, but we are supplied with plenty of fuel. There have been repeated orders given concerning the provision and regulation of batt horses for the ensuing campaign.

29th January—Several donation articles from our friends in England have been delivered out to us, which are very acceptable at this season; such as cloth trousers, flannel waistcoats, gloves, night-caps, socks, stockings, and two pair of shoes for each man.

CHAPTER 13

February 1794

6th February—In consequence of his Majesty's commands, his Royal Highness the commander in chief sets off for London.

The command of the British troops devolves on Lieutenant-General Sir William Erskine, during the absence of his Royal Highness.

9th February—Lieutenant-General Sir William Erskine in this day's orders announced to the troops the safe arrival of his Royal Highness the Duke of York in England.

10th February—Eight squadrons of cavalry under the command of Lieutenant-Colonel Stavely, with a field officer to each four squadrons, were ordered to be ready to march at the shortest notice, and to take three days bread and forage with them.

Our brigade was also ordered to be in readiness to march at the shortest notice, and each man to be furnished with sixty rounds of ammunition.

Likewise the different battalion guns, with eight pieces of cannon in reserve.

The signal for the troops at Tembling was to be three guns fired from the grand parade.

During the absence of the troops under orders for marching, the main guard, and the prisoners guard were to be taken by such of the cavalry and artillery as remained behind.

All this was on account of some threatening appearance of the enemy, but as they made no farther attempt, our preparation was consequently dropt.

15th February—This day a detachment from the brigade of guards, consisting of 800 men, with four twelve pounders, and two howitzers, were ordered to march to-morrow morning at nine o'clock towards Courtray, and to put themselves under the command of General Abercrombie. The detachment had orders to take three days bread and forage with them, with their camp equipage. The above detachment to be commanded by Colonel Drummond of the 1st guards, etc.

16th February—The detachments marched as ordered, and on the 18th arrived at Courtray, where they were lodged in the barracks.

20th February—Part of the detachment relieved the Imperial troops at the posts of Marke, Lowe, Albeck, etc. This relief consisted of about 400 men.

Our advanced posts at present reach from Menin eastward, by Hollingham, Tourcoign, Rubaix, Lannoy, to Cysoign.

21st February—The British troops in Courtray consist of the detachments from the brigade of guards, the 37th regiment of foot, two regiments of light cavalry, *viz.* the 7th and 15th, with several battalions of the foreign troops.

24th February—This afternoon a body of French cavalry, to appearance about 200, advanced on our piquets stationed on the Lille great road, but upon our patrols falling back they retired.

The French have broke up the pavement of the road leading to Lille, and also cut the trees down and laid them across it.

The whole brigade now arrived at Courtray from Ghent, with the other troops, etc.

CHAPTER 14

March 1794

1st March—This morning about half past six o'clock, a heavy cannonade commenced towards Werwick and Lincelles, which two places the allied troops from Menin attacked and drove the French out of them. About ten o'clock the firing ceased.

2nd March—Our advanced posts are relieved every four days from the grand piquet at Marke, and the whole from Courtray every sixteen days.

8th March—Several movements took place among the troops, in changing their stations, etc. This afternoon a detachment from the brigade of guards, of 300 men, marched from Courtray, under the command of a field officer, in order to support the Hessians, should they have been attacked, they having advanced their main piquet from Marke to Lauwe.

9th March—A draught from England of 750 men joined the brigade of guards this day, preparatory to the ensuing campaign.

11th March—This morning a heavy firing was heard towards Lincelles and Werwick, which proved to be an attempt the enemy had made on our advanced posts, under the cover of the darkness of the morning. They obliged our posts to retire, but were repulsed afterwards, with very small loss.

12th March—Some firing of musketry this morning at the advanced posts.

13th March—The detachment at Marke was relieved by another of the same strength from the brigade guards. Major-general Lake arrived at Courtray this day.

18th March—This afternoon a French hussar deserted to us, and brought with him his horse, arms, and accoutrements.

Every preparation is making for opening the campaign.

22nd March—All the heavy baggage, spare tents, and every thing not absolutely necessary for our use, was sent back to Ghent, and a sergeant of each battalion appointed to take charge of it.

Several sick men who are not able to march are also sent along with it.

26th March—We began our march towards the opening of the campaign, about seven o'clock in the morning, and marched to the village of Peck, when the army halted and was quartered in the neighbouring farms and villages.

27th March—Marched about six o'clock from the village of Peck, and passing through Tournay, reached St. Amand about four o'clock in the afternoon, when the 1st and 3rd regiments were lodged in the convent; the flank battalion of Coldstream was quartered in the neighbouring villages, but removed into the town of St. Amand a few days after, and quartered there.

This ancient town has no very fine appearance in itself, although the situation is very pleasant, on the river Scarpe, which winds slowly through the neighbouring woods and meadows, and falls into the Scheldt near the hill of Maulde.

The church is the principal curiosity in it, being a stately building, with a lofty steeple of very curious architecture, but now neglected and falling into decay, being used for a magazine for hay, corn, etc. for the army. The convent adjoining is also a spacious building, and in the days of its prosperity has had few equals, but is now totally neglected. Here the army are lodged upon all emergencies in passing through, there being sufficient room in the spacious apartments and galleries for one thousand men.

How would the bigots of superstition, in former days, have thundered forth their anathemas against him who durst pollute their holy place in such a manner, whilst they, under the veil of sanctity, polluted it far worse with their lustful abominations, with the beautiful but deluded daughters of their country. Upon the whole, the church and convent being joined in one, has an appearance of awful grandeur, and looks "Majestic tho' in ruins."

Near the church is a small marketplace, with a fountain in the middle of it. They have lately built a church of brick, in a plain modern taste, the walls of which bear the marks of the French cannon, when they were driven out by the General Clairfait last year. Several of the houses in the street leading to Valenciennes gate, are entirely demolished by them, as they generally endeavoured to destroy what they could not possess.

30th March—The soldiers of the brigade of guards, who were present in the glorious action at Lincelles, the 18th of August, 1793, received a reward for their gallantry on that occasion; it was paid in the following proportion, *viz*:

	£	s	d
A sergeant	1	1	0
A corporal		14	3
A drummer and private soldier, each		9	9

His Royal Highness the commander in chief having previously ordered a board of general officers to assemble, in order to consider of and determine a compensation to be made to the officers, non-commission officers, and soldiers of the

British army, for the losses sustained in the retreat from Dunkirk last year. The board having come to a determination, and his Royal Highness approved of it, the following sums were paid to those entitled to receive them, proper certified returns having been previously given in, *viz*:

		£	s	d
Colonel	Baggage	120	0	0
	Camp equipage	80	0	0
Field Officer	Baggage	10	0	0
	Camp equipage	60	0	0
Captain	Baggage	80	0	0
	Camp equipage	35	0	0
Subaltern	Baggage	–	–	–
	Camp equipage	–	–	–
Quartermaster	Baggage	–	–	–
	Camp equipage	27	10	0

The above is the allowance made for the whole, and so in proportion for any part of it

		£	s	d
A sergeant of infantry	For the whole of his necessaries	2	10	0
	For three-quarters ditto	1	17	6
	and so on in proportion			
A private soldier	Whole	2	2	0
	For three-quarters	1	11	6
	For one-half	1	1	0
	For one-fourth		10	6

The sergeants and privates of the cavalry were allowed a trifle more than the infantry; and an officer's servant, for the whole of his necessaries, £3, and so in proportion for any part of it.

There are also new tents of a round form, and superior quality to the old ones, each tent is to contain sixteen men; also new kettles, two to each tent, with a horse per company to carry them, which is a great convenience to the soldiers, nothing being more irksome on a long march than carrying a kettle.

CHAPTER 15
April 1794

Early April—A general court martial sat here on a soldier of the 24th regiment of foot, accused of murdering an inhabitant of the country, a man dwelling at a small distance from here, on the banks of the Scarpe. But though there was no reason to doubt his being guilty, the court could not find themselves justified in condemning him to suffer death; but sentenced him to a thousand lashes.

In this instance, as well as many others of late, justice loudly calls for some singular example; for notwithstanding repeated orders, and severe threatenings, time after time, pillaging, and lawless depredations are still practised in some part of the army or other.

His Royal Highness informed the army of the above affair in the following manner in public orders:

Head Quarters
St. Amand
31st March, 1794

Parole Stanislaus

It is with the utmost concern that the commander in chief announces to the army, that he has received a report that three British soldiers, dressed in great coats, and with leather caps on, similar to those worn by the light infantry, went yesterday into a house, in the village of Warlem, which they plundered, and on the owner remonstrating with them, and saying he would complain to the General, one of the men drew a pistol and shot him; the man died of his wounds this morning.

His Royal Highness is convinced, that it is not necessary for him to make any observation on a conduct so atrocious and disgraceful, to induce all persons under his command to use their utmost efforts to detect and bring to punishment the perpetrators of this act: he, however, thinks proper to promise a reward of thirty guineas to any person who can give such information as will lead to a discovery; and if it is a soldier who gives such information, he will receive his discharge should he require it.

His Royal Highness is pleased further to offer the same terms, together with a free pardon to either of the men concerned, who will turn King's evidence, and prosecute to conviction; with an exception only to the actual perpetrator of the murder.

These orders to be read at the head of every troop and company, at roll-call, two successive days.

Each man was also furnished by the Duke's recommendation, at the expense of our friends in England, with a great coat of strong grey cloth, made after the Austrian fashion, which proves of infinite service to us, both on duty and off.

9th April—This day a general movement took place in the army, which took up cantonments at Famars, and the villages and places adjacent.

The brigade of guards marched to St. Leger, a straggling village on the river Scheldt, above Valenciennes, where we took up quarters for this night.

10th April—Passed the Scheldt at Frith, with a number of

other corps, and marched to Vendegies sur l'Ecaillon, a re-markable dirty straggling village, where we remained can-toned till every thing was prepared and ready for the field.

Yesterday two soldiers of the 14th regiment of foot, fol-lowing up their usual practice of plundering the poor inhab-itants, entered a house, and on the people attempting to make some resistance in defence of their little all, the villains, with unfeeling barbarity, murdered the mother, and wounded her infant in such a manner that it died soon after.

The following is his Royal Highness's address to the army upon the occasion:

Famars
April 10th, 1794

Parole Bernardino

His Royal Highness the commander in chief earnestly requests, that the general and field officers, captains, and officers commanding companies, will take pains to ex-plain to the men of the army under their command, the following order, addressed in a particular manner to the private men of the army:

> His Royal Highness feels it to be unnecessary that he should seek for any other than the plainest and most direct language, to convey to them the sentiments under the impression of which it was dictated.
> His Royal Highness therefore announces his full determination, to exert every effort of severity and rigour, to put a stop to the scenes of plunder and outrage, of which so many instances have lately occurred, to the dishonour of the British army.
> Major-General Abercrombie reported yesterday to his Royal Highness, that two men of the 14th regiment had, during the preceding evening, at-tempted to rob the house of a countryman, that in the course of the attempt, they had murdered

the woman of the house, and that a child had also been so much wounded, that there was little hopes of its living.

His Royal Highness leaves it to those amongst the class of his brother soldiers, whom he now addresses, and in whose minds there exist those principles of honour and integrity, which can alone render them worthy the appeal, and which he trusts and believes is by far the greater number of them, to judge of the feelings which must have forced themselves upon his mind, at receiving a report of an act so atrocious and inhuman in its nature, and so well calculated to cast the most injurious stigma on the national character in general, and that of the army under his immediate command in particular.

His Royal Highness is persuaded, that there can be but one sentiment of detestation and horror upon the occasion, and he relies so much upon this conviction, that he forbears, as unnecessary, to make any further observations upon it.

His Royal Highness feels himself called upon, by every tie of justice, humanity, and duty, to punish, by a single act of severity, the perpetrators of so horrid a fact. Under this impression he did not hesitate a moment to order the Provost to proceed to the spot, and by the instant execution of the offenders, to make atonement to the violated laws of God and man, and endeavour by that terror, which he is convinced can alone have any effect upon minds lost to every feeling of religion, humanity, and honour, to put a stop to a conduct, of which too many instances have of late occurred, to leave his Royal Highness any doubt of the necessity of an immediate and rigorous interference.

(The two men were executed this morning at the head of the brigade.)

> His Royal Highness trusts the army will do him the justice to believe, that it was not without the utmost regret and concern, that he thus gave way to the necessity which urged him to doom two of his fellow creatures to so awful a fate, which they indeed too well merited. It was the future advantage of the army, and the hope that such an act of severity would render a repetition of it unnecessary, which alone actuated his Royal Highness to depart from the ordinary proceedings of justice. He most earnestly and ardently prays, that it may have the effect which he had in view.
>
> At the same time he repeats his full determination to persist in the exercise of the most rigorous means in the discharge of the duty which he owes to God, to his King, and to his Country, and to the brave and good of the army which it will be his pride to command, only while by its conduct it may merit the general approbation of our country, as much as he is sure it will at all times by its courage.

This is in general an open country, pleasantly variegated with hills and valleys, but not in a very good state of cultivation. Both beef and mutton are very plenty, and reasonable.

14th April—His Imperial Majesty having signified his intention of reviewing all the troops composing the army on the heights above Cateau, the 16th instant, those under the immediate command of his Royal Highness the Duke of York are ordered to assemble on the heights above Bormerain at nine o'clock that morning. The several brigades, with the reserve artillery, to march in several columns from their present quarters. The officers commanding are desired to examine

89

the roads to-morrow, and ascertain the distance, as they are desired to compass their march, so as to arrive at Bormerain precisely at the hour appointed.

Further directions will be given at Bormerain for forming the columns of march from thence to Cateau.

Here some of our battalions were furnished with straps, for the purpose of carrying our great coats, flung across the shoulders, neatly rolled up. This, in all sorts of weather, was part of our equipment.

16th April—According to the orders of the 14th, the several corps of the army under the command of his Royal Highness the Duke of York, assembled at 9 o'clock in the morning on the heights of Bormerain, and from thence proceeded in several columns to the heights of Cateau, where we found the Emperor's troops already assembled. It was a fine day, and the sun shone clear, which contributed much to the good appearance of the troops; there was line after line, and column after column, extended over all the heights.

About six o'clock the Emperor attended with a long retinue, rode briskly along the lines, but had not time to take notice of every distinct corps.

After he had passed our brigade, we moved forward, crossing the Cambray high road, within a mile of Cateau; it being now dark, we could see the latter town finely illuminated, on account of the Emperor and the Duke of York lodging there. We soon reached our appointed place, and pitched our tents for the first time this campaign in some fields of wheat. We had been previously ordered to have, two days provisions ready cooked with us, which saved us the trouble now of dressing it.

17th April—About eight o'clock this morning the whole combined army was in motion, and a glorious sight it was to see, the vast extended columns of cavalry, infantry, and artillery, moving in different directions, according to the plan of attack.

A Sergeant of the Coldstream Guards

The Emperor and his army turned off, to the left, towards Landrecy, where they soon drove in the out-posts, and laid siege to it. While we were on the march, we could see a good deal of cannonading on our left towards the Sambre, above Landrecy.

But now came our turn to exhibit; our principal attack was intended against a village called Vaux, near which place the enemy had strengthened themselves considerably, and thrown up a redoubt around a windmill, in which they had five pieces of cannon, with either one or two mortars. This post had an exceeding fine command, and as soon as the head of our column advanced within shot, they began a heavy cannonade; but it is to be observed, that in this part of the country are many hollow ways, resembling the bed of a river dried up, which run with irregular windings through all the open country. In one of these hollow ways, directly in front of their battery, but at a considerable distance, our brigade formed the line of battle, and halted, while several pieces of cannon were detached round to the right near the edge of a wood, and brought to bear on the enemy with good effect. The French finding where we were drawn up, kept firing with the utmost vigour, but without effect, as we were un-der cover, except two spent balls, which sloping down the bank, went directly through the ranks, killed two men, broke the colour staff of the 3rd regiment in the ensign's hand, and wounded five more.

The hollow way where we stood took its course round to the left a considerable way, and came up to the village of Vaux, which lay behind the battery. We now marched round this way, following two grenadier companies of the 1st regiment, and the corps of O'Donnel, which had been led up towards the vil-lage, with an intent to storm the redoubt, but before we could reach it, the French had made good their retreat, and had also got their guns clear off, except one six pounder, which we sup-pose they had not horses to take away, as two lay dead in the redoubt, with a number of both killed and wounded men.

As they retreated, they were pursued through the wood of Leisse towards Bohain, by some Hessian light cavalry, who killed a great number.

They had the precaution to defend the wood, which lay on our right as we advanced to Vaux, both with cavalry and infantry, and also by felling trees across every pass, otherwise their retreat to Bohain must have been cut off.

After gaining possession of the redoubt, the 3rd regiment and Coldstream remained there, and the flank battalion and 1st regiment marched about two miles, where they halted as an advanced piquet towards Bohain. The night was very wet and cold, and we had no tents, as our baggage did not come up.

Some of the Austrian troops set most part of the village of Vaux on fire, which burnt almost all night. The Duke who had taken up his quarters there, was forced to leave them on account of the fire.

How wonderfully are some men's hearts hardened, and proof against every emotion of pity or humanity! Such are those who with wanton cruelty destroy in an hour what a poor inoffensive industrious family has toiled hard for years to obtain; and when they see the screaming, terrified children, hanging round their distressed mother, now left without a home, a prey to hunger, nakedness, and perhaps death, instead of moving their pity, it only provokes their scorn and abuse.

18th April—The whole of the Duke's column marched this morning (except the advanced guard, *viz.* the flank and 1st battalion of the guards, and the Inniskilling dragoons) and encamped on the heights between Basuiou and Catillon, a few miles south-east of Cateau.

The other two battalions of guards, with the Inniskilling, etc. advanced in the morning through the wood of Leisse, and formed a line close against the town of Bohain, while a reconnoitring party went in, but the French troops were all got clear off. The party was informed that the enemy fled with such precipitation, that they left their baggage, etc. in the town, but finding they were not pursued, returned back about midnight and took it away.

We then returned back again to Vaux, where we remained all night.

One part of the forest through which we passed and re-passed this morning, was strewed thick with dead bodies, killed in the pursuit of the cavalry yesterday, the greatest part of them had been killed with the sword, and were much mangled and cut in different places.

One of the above corpses drew the attention of a great number of people, on account of the beauty and whiteness of its skin; it lay in a ploughed field, was stripped naked, except the shirt, and appeared to have been a youth of about eighteen or nineteen years of age, of the most exact proportion of shape and size, a skin perfectly clear and white, without the smallest spot or blemish, except where he had been wounded: he had received a shot in the groin, and a cut through his left eye, very deep.

19th April—The two battalions at Vaux being relieved by Major-General Abercrombie's corps, marched by a wide circuitous route to the place where the rest of the brigade were encamped; but not halting there, continued our route through Cateau, about two miles along the Cambray road, that being the position designed for our army to take, in order to cover the siege of Landrecy, and also to watch the motions of the enemy near Cambray.

The two battalions encamped near Catillon, with the rest of the troops there, joined us, and took up their new encampment.

20th April—His Royal Highness addressed the troops on the action of the 17th:

Head Quarters
Cateau
April 19, 1794

His Royal Highness the Duke of York takes the earliest opportunity of testifying the sense he entertains of the bravery and conduct of the troops which composed the two columns under his immediate command in the very extensive operations of the 17th instant; his personal observation of the spirit and steadiness with which the officers and men of the column which attacked the enemy's entrenchments on the heights above Vaux, and in the wood of Bohain, supported a very severe cannonade; and the report made to him by Sir William Erskine that the same qualities were equally displayed by his column at the attack of the enemy's works at Fremont, calls upon him to express to them his warmest approbation.

The companies of O'Donald, which led the attack of the redoubt; the two companies of grenadiers of the 1st regiment of British guards which supported that attack; the three battalions of Austrian grenadiers commanded by Major-General Petrash, who forced the enemy in the wood; and the hussars of Arch Duke Ferdinand, with a squadron of the 16th light dragoons, under Major Lapport, who turned their right; as well as those who under their brave leader, Colonel Davey, so gallantly pursued on the left, are all entitled to his best acknowledgments; as are in an equal manner the three battalions of the regiment of Kaunitz, who, by the report of Sir William Erskine, attacked the works of the enemy at Fremont with the intrepidity which at all times distinguishes the Austrian troops.

His Royal Highness desires in a particular manner to offer his best thanks to Lieutenant-Generals Sir William Erskine and Otto, for the judgment and good conduct which they so conspicuously displayed in the discharge of their respective duties.

To Major-General Abercrombie, for the zeal, activity, and spirit with which he led the advanced guard of his column; and to Lieutenant-Colonel Count Murfield, of the Etat-major, for the very great and active assistance which his Royal Highness derived from his abilities.

His Royal Highness desires that Captain Boag and Lieutenant Page of the royal artillery will accept his thanks for the very spirited and able manner with which they conducted the battery entrusted to their care.

The following order was issued the same day, by order of His Imperial Majesty and the Duke of York:

All persons are forbid, upon pain of death, the pillaging or burning of houses or villages, as by those means we lose all the necessaries and comforts of them.

The following order issued the same day, shows the care and attention of our royal commander towards the lives and property of individuals:

By order of His Royal Highness the Duke of York, an officer and forty men of the guards to be immediately sent to Basuyaux, to enforce the order for preventing pillaging and burning houses, and the officer is to inform General Otto of his arrival there.

21st April—A working party, consisting of three subalterns, four sergeants, four corporals, and 300 men, was furnished by our brigade this day, for the purpose of throwing up redoubts and strengthening our position.

22nd April—The working parties continued; they are generally relieved twice in twenty-four hours, and work as long as they can see; they are paid at the rate of four pence *per diem*.

23rd April—A heavy cannonading heard from Landrecy, which the Emperor's troops are bombarding with the utmost vigour.

Our forage, wood, etc. is brought here from Englefontaine.

The British troops are here:

Cavalry	Major-General Sir R. Lawrie's brigade
	Colonel Vyses's brigade
	Major-General Mansell's
	Major-General Dundas's brigade
	Seventh
	First light dragoons
	Fifteenth light dragoons
	Sixteenth light dragoons
Infantry	Brigade of guards
	First brigade of the line
	Second brigade of the line

Besides artillery and the Austrians, Hessians, etc. consisting of artillery, cavalry, and infantry, composed above as many more.

24th April—This morning about four o'clock a column of the enemy, consisting of both cavalry and infantry, was discovered towards our right flank. That quarter being commanded by the Austrian General Otto, a gallant officer, our 15th light dragoons, and some Austrian hussars were ordered to charge them, which they did with such spirit and gallantry, that the French soon gave way, while our valiant dragoons pursued the flying foe near four miles, with great slaughter. Prisoners they took but few, as they employed their time to a better purpose, namely, following up, and completing their victory.

The 15th light dragoons, and the hussars of Tuscany, were supported by two or three squadrons from the 1st dragoon guards, the blues, and Prince of Wales's; their loss was very small, the 15th and Prince of Wales's dragoons suffered most. The enemy lost above two hundred killed and wounded in the field, with nine pieces of cannon.

The engagement lasted about eight hours. In the afternoon

three battalions of the guards marched to the place which they had occupied, and remained there a few hours until all was quiet, and then returned to camp.

25th April—The siege of Landrecy is carrying on with the greatest activity; we hear a constant cannonade, and at night can see the shells frequently.

Three squadrons of cavalry and three battalions of infantry are in constant readiness night and day, to turn out in a moment: this duty is taken by rotation throughout the army. The whole line is also ready every morning at day-break.

26th April—The enemy, determined to make another effort in order to raise the siege of Landrecy, advanced this morning towards our encampment in five columns, drove in our out-posts, piquets, etc. and at six o'clock the heads of some of their columns were within cannon shot of our camp. The infantry were drawn up in front of their respective encampments, and the quarter guard tents struck, but no others were suffered to be touched, nor the least appearance of confusion. Several pieces of cannon were drawn forward just clear of the encampment, and a brisk cannonade began, which a little retarded their progress. Their left column, which it seems was the strongest, approached with great confidence, and we could observe the squadrons of cavalry and divisions of infantry advancing over a rising ground at a small distance with great rapidity.

And now every expectation was on the rack, awaiting some command that might determine an event that appeared so big with sudden fate.

At length the Duke, who from No. 1 redoubt (it being the highest) was watching all their proceedings, observed, that their left flank was not covered, on which he immediately ordered the following regiments of cavalry to advance and turn that flank, namely, the Austrian regiment of cuirassiers, Zetzwichtz, the blues, 1st, 3rd, and 5th dragoon guards, the royals, Arch-Duke Ferdinand's hussars, and the 16th light dragoons.

These accordingly advanced with cool deliberate valour, and turning the enemy's flank, amidst showers of grape shot and musketry, charged through their squadrons and battalions, backward and forward, bearing all down before them with irresistible force. We could observe from the camp several of our squadrons charging through the French cavalry, then through a battalion of infantry, after which they would wheel round, and charge back again in the same manner, so that it was impossible for the enemy to rally or collect their terrified troops.

The 7th and 11th light dragoons in the mean time were performing prodigies of valour on the left, while our artillery advanced in front, and added to the general confusion of the French.

The overthrow now became universal, cavalry and infantry were thrown together in promiscuous heaps, or scattered in astonishment over the plains. The cavalry that were left now took to their heels and fled, pursued with terror to the very gates of Cambray before they durst look behind. The infantry following their example, to facilitate their flight, threw away their knapsacks, arms, and accoutrements, and made the best of their way, leaving our brave dragoons absolute masters of the field.

But they did not all run away who came that morning, the fields were covered with the slain, and in some places they lay in heaps, with a considerable number of our gallant heroes among them. We also took near 3000 prisoners, and about fifty pieces of cannon, with the general who commanded them, General Chapuy.

We had the misfortune to lose Major-General Mansel, he was killed at the first onset.

In consequence of the above victory, the following order was issued this evening:

26th April, 1795

Pass Orders

In consequence of orders received from his Imperial Majesty, his Royal Highness the commander in chief, orders the troops to be under arms at the head of their respective encampments to-morrow morning at half past seven o'clock, to fire a *feu-de-joie*. The firing begins with the British reserve artillery, follows the Austrian artillery, and then the line from the right.

The men to be provided with three blank cartridges for the purpose.

27th April—The siege of Landrecy is carried on with great activity, though the besieged continue to make a vigorous defence.

The following is his Royal Highness's address to the army:

Head Quarters
Cateau
28th April, 1794
His Royal Highness, the commander in chief, has the highest satisfaction in congratulating the army on the glorious success of the 26th instant, in which the enemy, using every effort in a general attack, conducted in five columns for the relief of Landrecy, were repulsed in all of them, with a very great slaughter, and the loss of near fifty pieces of cannon.

The army under the immediate command of his Royal Highness bore a very conspicuous share in the signal success of the day, and his Royal Highness feels it incumbent on him to make his acknowledgments to those brave officers and soldiers, to whose valour and conduct, under the Divine direction, this great and important victory is to be ascribed.

To Lieutenant-General Otto, and to Colonel the Prince

of Swantzenbourg, to whose lot it fell to conduct the principal operations of the day, his Royal Highness desires to offer his best thanks, as well as to Colonel Vyse, who, on the misfortune of General Mansel, took the command of, and so gallantly led to the charge, two brigades of British cavalry.

His Royal Highness farther desires, that Major Brigade Payne and Captain Beckworth may know, that their conduct has been particularly mentioned to him by Prince Swantzenbourg, as highly meritorious.

The Austrian regiment of cuirassiers, Zetzwichtz, the blues, 1st, 3rd, and 5th dragoon guards, the royals, Arch-Duke Ferdinand's hussars, and the 16th light dragoons, who attacked and defeated the principal column of the enemy on the right, have all acquired immortal honour to themselves.

Nor is the determined gallantry with which, regardless of their number, the 7th and 11th light dragoons attacked the enemy on the left, less worthy of every commendation.

His Royal Highness requests, that the officers and men of those brave corps will accept of his thanks, and he desires they will be assured that he has not failed to represent their merits in the strongest terms to their respective sovereigns.

His Royal Highness is extremely desirous, that in the admiration excited by the success of the 26th, the less brilliant, though not less meritorious services of the light troops under General Otto, on the 24th instant, may not be overlooked. On that occasion, the conduct of the hussars, and 15th light dragoons, is particularly noticed on the report of Lieutenant-General Otto.

His Royal Highness has at all times had the highest confidence in the courage of the British troops in general, and he trusts that the cavalry will now be convinced, that wherever they attack with the firmness, velocity, and order which they showed upon this occasion, no numbers of the enemy we have to deal with, can resist them.

The late Major-General Mansel was buried at six o'clock this evening, in the redoubt No. 1. The corpse was preceded by three squadrons of his late brigade, and two pieces of cannon. The latter fired thirteen guns, at minute intervals, immediately after the interment. Major-Generals Abercrombie, Lake, Dundas, White, Fox, and Colonel D'Oyly, attended as pall-bearers, with the Duke and a great number of other officers.

29th April—This day the garrison of Landrecy surrendered to the Imperial army after a siege of nine days. The troops are to march out to-morrow morning without their arms, officers excepted, who are allowed to wear swords.

30th April—The enemy pressing hard upon General Clairfait, who commanded in West Flanders, it was deemed necessary to send some part of the army to his assistance; accordingly orders were issued this after-noon for the whole of the troops to be in readiness to march this evening at nine o'clock, in consequence of which the tents were struck, the baggage loaded, and every thing ready for marching at the hour appointed. Our route was for the camp at Famars, but we did not move off our ground before eleven o'clock, when we proceeded in the following order, *viz*:

Two squadrons 15th light dragoons
Six squadrons of the brigade, late Gen. Mansel's
Four battalions British guards
Two battalions Winsel Coloredo
Three battalions Austrian grenadiers
Six squadrons Colonel Vyse's brigade

The remainder of the troops on the advanced posts marched by another route to the same place, under the command of General Otto.

CHAPTER 16

May 1794

1st May—About noon we arrived at Famars, where we were ordered to halt for the space of four hours to refresh the troops who were much fatigued with their night's march. During our halt here, a heavy storm of rain fell, accompanied with thunder and lightning. At four o'clock we again resumed our march, and passed the Scheldt at Frith, through St. Leger, and from thence to the high road that leads from Valenciennes to St. Amand, which place it was intended we should reach that night; but the evening coming on, with a continued heavy rain, accompanied at short intervals with dreadful flashes of lightning, it became so excessive dark, that no one could perceive whether that next him was a man, a horse, or a wagon, of course every thing ran foul of each other; men and horses fell in the ditches together, and the drivers of the guns were forced to grope the way before their horses. In this situation, our brigade reached a straggling village, on the road between Valenciennes and the Abby de Vicoigne, where every one shifted for himself, and got under cover for the remainder of the night. General Lake and his horse both fell into a dangerous hole, the horse got out safe, but the General was much bruised.

2nd May—The brigade of guards marched into St. Amand this morning, and was ordered to their former lodging and quarters.

The commander in chief desires, that the officers commanding brigades will have distributed to their men a full allowance of rum for this day, which his Royal Highness will pay for.

3rd May—Marched about seven o'clock this morning, and at six o'clock in the evening arrived at our destined post, near Marquain, on the west of Tournay, much fatigued with these long marches.

4th May—The advanced posts are placed as formerly under the command of Lieutenant-General Otto, and consist of six squadrons of cavalry, supported by three battalions of infantry, which are relieved daily.

The following allowance of wood was ordered to be made to general officers, their suite, and officers of the staff:

Lieutenant-Generals and suite	30 rations of 12 pounds each for four days
Major-Generals and suite	20 rations of 12 pounds each for four days
Colonels	15 rations of 12 pounds each for four days
Field Officers	10 rations of 12 pounds each for four days
Captains	7 rations of 12 pounds each for four days
Subalterns	4 rations of 12 pounds each for four days

Major-Generals if in camp are allowed a proportion equal to that for 30 men
Colonels and Field Officers if in camp are allowed a proportion equal to that for 20 men

Captains, Subalterns, and Staff Officers if in camp are allowed a proportion equal to that for 10 men

10th May—About three o'clock this morning the enemy attacked our advanced posts, drove them in, and approached our encampment with great rapidity; we were immediately ordered under arms, and our tents struck, by that means if possible to draw them into a general engagement, but our cavalry drove them back again, killed a great number, and took prisoners

11th May—In this day's orders the Duke returned thanks to the corps engaged yesterday in the following manner:

His Royal Highness the commander in chief desires that Lieutenant-General Harcourt, Major-General Dundas, and Sir Robert Laurie, with the officers and men of the several corps of cavalry which were engaged yesterday, will accept his best thanks for the further proof which they gave of that spirit and conduct which his Royal Highness is well assured will ever be attended with the success it so well merits.

12th May—Extract from the orders of this day:

Head Quarters
Tournay
12th May, 1794
Parole Albertus
All pieces of ordnance, colours, tumbrels, and horses taken from the enemy, are to be delivered to the British artillery, and receipts taken for the same; which receipts, accompanied by a written application from the officer commanding the regiment who took them, are within three days to be sent to Mr. Commissary Williamson, who, by order of his Royal Highness the commander in chief, will pay the following rewards, *viz*:

	£
For each cannon or howitzer	20
For each pair of colours	10
For each tumbrel	10
For each horse	12

14th May—Every gun and wagon of the park of artillery, etc. were ordered to be provided with two fascines, being designed for the purpose of occasionally filling up, and repairing of bad passes on the road.

16th May—The army was ordered to cook two days provision, by which we knew some expedition was intended, which was no less than a general attack to be made by our whole army on the enemy, in the following order.

The army was divided into five columns, the two on the left were to force the passages of the river Marque, at Pont à Treflin, Willem, etc. and check the enemy at Lille. The centre column, which was composed of the brigade of guards, 1st brigade of the line, the free corps of O'Donnel, some of the British light cavalry, artillery, etc. was to force the enemy's post at Lannoy, and then proceed to Roubaix, etc. The next which was commanded by General Otto, was to proceed through Lurs, Waterloos, etc. to Tourcoing. The column on the right was to proceed through several intermediate places to Mouscron; and by this disposition it was intended to cut off the communication of the enemy's main army from Lille.

Every thing being ready, the tents were struck about nine o'clock this evening, and with the heavy baggage sent off to a place behind Tournay.

About eleven o'clock the army was in motion. Our column was commanded by Major-general Abercrombie, but the Duke accompanied it; as being the centre of the army, it was the most convenient place for him to receive information, or give orders.

17th May—The morning being very hazy, we halted near the village of Templeuve, till about nine o'clock, when we moved forwards towards Lannoy, which, after a brisk cannonade for a short time, the enemy abandoned.

In this attack Major Wright of the royal artillery was mortally wounded, and died soon after. This is a remarkably fatal place for the officers of our artillery, one being killed and two wounded here last year.

We then after a short halt proceeded towards Roubaix; a company of light infantry under the command of Lieutenant-Colonel Perryn, scouring the left flank all the way. The enemy made a stout opposition at Roubaix, and after their out-posts were drove in, answered our cannon for some time with great spirit, and then retreated, getting clear off with all their guns. We then entered the town in triumph after a little difficulty, they having cut down a number of trees across the road near the entrance. Many of the inhabitants were fled, and left their homes shut up, and those who remained, eyed us with a kind of vacant look, hardly knowing whether to esteem us as friends or foes.

The brigade of the line was posted on the *chaussee* leading from Roubaix to Lille, to prevent a surprise from that quarter; and the brigade of guards were drawn up in the field on the west side of the town; there they refreshed themselves with what they had with them, and were also supplied plentifully with several articles from the town.

Roubaix is a handsome town, laying with a gentle declivity towards the south, on which side runs a small rivulet, winding through the meadows. In the marketplace was erected the tree of liberty, impaled round with the red cap on the top of it, which our men soon levelled with the ground.

About sun-set General Abercrombie received orders to attack Mouvaux, a village two miles distant, strongly situated by nature, and surrounded with palisadoes and entrenchments, together with several flanking redoubts.

We accordingly advanced to the attack with great vigour and alacrity, from the refreshment we had received at Roubaix, and after some time spent in cannonading, the flank battalion which had been in front all day, having formed the line, and advancing towards the enemy, eagerly catched the word "charge," and rushed with the utmost. impetuosity into the enemy's works, upon which they fled with the greatest precipitation, leaving behind them three pieces of cannon, In the mean time the light cavalry wheeling round the village, overtook them in their flight, and pursued them about three miles with great slaughter.

After taking possession of the village, piquets were sent out wherever they were deemed necessary, and the remainder betook themselves to rest, highly pleased with the glorious success of the day.

It is a happy thing for us mortals that we cannot see into futurity, otherwise we would certainly overlook all our blessings and enjoyments, and fix all our thoughts with fearful expectation on the approach of each calamity.

If we had known, however, what our next day's work was to be, we should not at least have slept so sound that night.

It happened unfortunately that our column was the only one that was successful in the general attack of yesterday. The two columns on our left were either repulsed at the Marque, or so matched, that they could advance no farther, consequently our left flank was left open to the numberless legions that poured out from Lille.

18th May—The column on the right was defeated, and forced to fall back again.

General Otto's column on our right gained its point, and took possession of Tourcoign, but could not keep it, being driven out again and forced to retreat, so that we were left exposed on all sides.

The morning was ushered in by a tremendous cannonade in the woods near Tourcoign, on our right, where the Austrians were forced to fall back; then towards Roubaix, behind us, where our brigade of the line were forced to give way; then on our left, where our piquets were drove in; and before us, multitudes of both cavalry and infantry appeared, advancing in all directions.

It was now about nine o'clock, and our brave general being apprized of our real situation, with respect to the other parts of the army, and having no prospect of any assistance being sent him, ordered us to retreat.

Accordingly we marched back towards Roubaix, with the

artillery and the main body of the brigade, while the skirmishing parties all around us made it appear like a kind of running fight. On coming near the town, we found the enemy assembled in great numbers in the wood to the right of the town, from whence they would have annoyed us greatly on our entrance; we therefore made a halt, and with four twelve pounders being drawn up, gave them such a salute as made them sheer off. We then proceeded through the town, which the front of the column cleared very well; but before the rear got clear of the gate, the enemy pressed very hard upon them, both with grape shot and musketry, and killed and wounded a great many.

On gaining the summit of the hill, after passing the town, a short halt was made, in order to collect the troops more close together, or see if any thing could be done; but the enemy pressing in on all sides, in such superior numbers, it was thought vain to attempt any thing offensive; we therefore moved on again, in hopes of reaching Lannoy, amid volleys of round and grape shot from all quarters. At every avenue, or pass, they had guns to flank us, and their cavalry were ready whenever the ground would admit them to act.

Thus we went, beset on all sides, for upwards of three miles. Immediately after our last formation, a squadron or two of some foreign hussars, instead of endeavouring to check the enemy, rode away at full speed, even through the midst of our own men, if they chanced to be in their way, and added confusion to confusion. The most part of our officers batt horses and others were so frightened at the shot, that they became quite unmanageable, and throwing off their loads, ran with the utmost fury up and down, among the soldiers.

The women also, who inadvertently had been permitted to follow us, caused no small disorder; some being killed, others wounded, and some loaded with plunder, so as to be unable to keep up with the men.

It was now discovered that Lannoy was in possession of

the enemy, and our flank battalion guns being advanced too far in front, without a proper support, a strong detachment of cavalry from Lannoy met and took them, with all the men, except one, prisoners.

We were now forced to leave the road, and make our way through the fields between Lannoy and Leers: this was another occasion of our losing some more of our guns and tumbrels, not being able to get them over the hedges and ditches through which we passed.

In the mean time our British light cavalry, which were with us, performed wonders of valour, charging the enemy with unexampled courage, wherever they approached: it was no uncommon thing to see one of them attack three of the French dragoons at once, in order to rescue the prisoners they were carrying off.

It was owing to their bravery that so few prisoners were taken, as well as the great numbers which they retook from the enemy.

As soon as we reached the village of Templeuve, we halted and formed; and from thence marched to our former position behind the village of Blandin, with very different sensations from what we had the evening before.

Our loss proved to be very inconsiderable to what might have been expected in such a situation; for it was rather to be wondered at that one of us escaped.

The flank battalions in the several attacks of the 17th instant, had seven rank and file killed; two officers, *viz.* Colonel Manners, and Colonel Ludlow, and thirty-three rank and file wounded.

The brigade of the line under the command of Major-General Fox suffered very severely.

The 3rd regiment of guards also lost one of their colours, not taken by the enemy, but through the careless misconduct of a sergeant.

Return of the Killed, Wounded, and Missing of the Brigade of Foot Guards on the 17th and 18th of May, 1794

	Capt.		Lieut.		Sergt.		Drum.		R & F		
	Killed	Wounded	Killed	Wounded	Killed	Wounded	Killed	Wounded	Killed	Wounded	Missing
Flank Battalion	2		1		1				12	51	13
1st Regiment									6	8	6
Coldstream	1						1			5	3
3rd Regiment					1				2	9	14
Total	3		1		2		1		20	73	36

Flank Battalion	Colonel Manners	Wounded
	Lieutenant-Colonel Ludlow	Wounded
	Captain Drummond	Wounded
Coldstream	Lieutenant-Colonel Gascoyne	Wounded
1st Regiment	Mr Robinson, Surgeon	Taken Prisoner

19th May—Towards the evening we changed the position of our encampment, the British heavy cavalry and infantry taking their ground on the left of the line.

Head Quarters
Tournay
19th May, 1794
Parole Martinus
In noticing the event of yesterday, his Royal Highness the commander in chief finds little to regret but the loss of brave men, which, however, appears to be less, than from the nature of the action might have been expected.

The proximity of the enemy's garrisons and armies, the want of that complete success in the other parts of the intended operations, which would have secured the flanks of our position, and above all the nature of the country, so favourable to the kind of attack which the enemy undertook. These will sufficiently account for what has happened, without any imputation on the conduct and bravery of our troops; with them his Royal Highness has every reason to be perfectly satisfied, and he doubts not, but the enemy will feel to their cost, upon the first occasion which may present itself, to what they owe the advantage they have a had the good fortune to obtain yesterday, over troops as much superior to them in bravery and discipline, as is the cause we maintain to that for which they contend.

In fact, the enemy has little to boast of but the acquisition of some pieces of British artillery; which being the first that has fallen into their hands in the field, may afford matter of triumph; and though his Royal Highness regrets that they should have that to boast of, yet he is perfectly satisfied, that it is to be attributed to the difficulty of the country alone, and not to the smallest failure in the courage and conduct which was exerted to save them.

The corps to give in returns of their loss immediately, and his Royal Highness relies on the zeal and activity of the commanding officers, for repairing every thing that will admit of it, with the utmost dispatch, so that .they may want nothing essential for future service that can be procured them.

21st May—A detachment of two hundred grenadiers of the brigade of guards, with one captain, and four subalterns, attended the funeral of the late Major Wright, of the royal artillery, who died of the wounds he received on the 17th instant.

22nd May—This day the enemy having previously collected all their force, made a vigorous and general attack on our lines, in several columns; their greatest efforts were made on our right, near the river Scheldt, which also covered their left flank; they maintained their ground in that quarter with uncommon resolution, and with very little variation the whole day; having this particular advantage, that they were able from their vast numbers to pour in continual supplies of fresh troops to action; and also from the nature of the country and their situation, could change them with very little inconveniency.

A numerous column approached our lines, near the centre, through the villages of Templeuve and Blandin, but a redoubt having been thrown up near the road by which alone they could approach, and some other pieces of ordnance being placed a little to the left, in an advantageous situation, they were suffered to advance pretty near unmolested, when the whole opened upon them with such effect, that they were forced to retreat in, the utmost confusion, and with very great loss. Notwithstanding which they made two more spirited attempts to force that passage, but were repulsed with equal loss and confusion.

Meanwhile a column confirming of 5 or 6000 men made its appearance towards our left, on which account the brigade of guards and the British heavy cavalry remained ready for action on their camp ground all that day, (the baggage and camp equipage being sent away in the morning,) but they observing our advantageous situation, and dreading the thought of meeting the British cavalry a second time on an open plain, thought proper not to make any approaches.

About three o'clock in the afternoon, the right wing of our army being much fatigued, and having lost a great number of men, began to lose ground considerably, and the enemy having passed the village of Froiennes, in and near which the hottest of the action had continued the whole day, advanced fast towards Tournay on the Courtray road; on which his Royal Highness sent the second brigade of British infantry under the. command of Major-General Fox, it consisted of the 14th, 37th, and 53rd regiments, with some of the British artillery. This brigade meeting the enemy, after firing a few rounds, charged them with such resolution and, bravery, that it turned the scale of action once more in our favour, and the enemy were forced to fall back; and through the spirit and activity of our artillery, who also came fresh into action, they continued to lose ground, though but slowly till darkness

Impos'd a grateful truce,
And silence on the odious din of war.

Such a battle has, I believe, seldom been known, so fierce, and for such a length of time; our out-posts were driven in, and the cannonading begun at seven in the morning, and continued one continual roar of artillery and musketry till near half past nine at night.

It is said that the French had above one hundred thousand men this morning, and that they have left above 9000 dead in the field. Report says also, that our army had near 4000 men killed, besides a vast number wounded. We took seven pieces of cannon from them in the course of the day. The whole of the troops remained under arms all night, but when morning appeared, we perceived the enemy had retired.

23rd May—
Head Quarters
Tournay
23rd May, 1794

Parole Americus

It is his Royal Highness the commander in chief's express order, that whenever the troops, or any particular corps, march without their camp equipage, no woman is upon any pretence whatever to be permitted to follow the column.

His Royal Highness desires this may be considered as a standing order, and expects the commanding officers of regiments will take care it is most strictly complied with.

It is necessary at the same time to warn the women and followers of the army, that the provost-marshal is hereby directed to inflict on every offender the most exemplary punishment; and if the offence deserves it, even to execute on the spot, any woman or follower of the army, of any description whatever, who by cruelty, plunder, or marauding, may bring disgrace on the troops under his Royal Highness's command.

This order to be read at this evening's roll call, at the head of every troop or company in the army, on which occasion all women and followers of the army are ordered to attend, that none may plead ignorance of the awful punishment to which they will subject themselves by this crime. And his Royal Highness relies with confidence on the assistance of every officer to prevent the glory so justly acquired by the army in the field, being sullied by acts of inhumanity and depredation.

Whenever it is possible, it is the order of his Majesty the Emperor, that all attacks may be made with drums beating and colours flying.

His Majesty the Emperor has desired that his most particular thanks may be expressed to every part of the allied army that was engaged yesterday, for the great gallantry they displayed, by which the desirable end was obtained, of completely defeating the enemy.

His Royal Highness the commander in chief desires to express his particular thanks to Major-General Fox; to the 14th regiment under the command of Major Ramsy; to the 37th regiment commanded by Captain Lightburn; to the 53rd regiment commanded by Major Wiseman; and to the detachment of artillery that was attached to them under the command of Capt. Trotter; for that great display of intrepidity and good conduct which reflects the greatest honour upon themselves, at the same time that it was highly instrumental in deciding the important victory of the 22nd.

His Royal Highness much laments the loss they have sustained, but flatters himself they feel it in some manner compensated by the credit they have gained.

24th May—A malicious report having been circulated through the army, that it was owing to some misconduct in themselves, that the British troops were surrounded on the 18th instant, the Emperor published the following declaration:

Head Quarters
Tournay
24th May, 1794

Parole Christophules

His Imperial Majesty has heard with the greatest displeasure, that a report has been spread of the British troops having allowed themselves to be surprised on the 18th instant.

He hastens, therefore, to make it publicly known, that he is perfectly convinced of the untruth of this report, and of their having behaved that day with their accustomed resolution and courage; that they only retired from the too great superiority of the enemy's numbers, being attacked in front, flanks, and rear, at the same time; and that their retreat was performed with the utmost steadiness and order.

His Imperial Majesty takes the earliest opportunity to inform the troops of the combined powers, that since he has taken the command of the army, he has almost every day had proofs of their ardour and courage, and cannot too strongly express his satisfaction and gratitude to them on their former conduct.

26th May—Ever since we have taken this position we have had a great number of men employed at work.

A chain of redoubts runs all along the front and flanks of this extensive encampment from the Scheldt on the right to the Orchies road on the left, and so well calculated for defence, that we are under no apprehension of being taken by storm.

27th May—Several women that were taken prisoners on the 18th and carried into Lille, returned to camp. They are loud in praise of the French, whom they extol to the skies for their civility and kindness to them, and the rest of the prisoners; they say they were loaded with wine and other provisions, and accompanied to the gates of Lille with a band of music, and, from thence conducted to the advanced posts.

They brought several letters from the prisoners at Lille.

CHAPTER 17

June 1794

Early June—Extract from this day's orders:

Corps to give a return to-morrow morning at orderly time, to the quartermaster-general, of the names of the women in each, whose husbands have been killed or taken prisoners, and who are desirous of going to England.

4th June—Anniversary of his Majesty's birth-day, his Royal Highness gave an entertainment, to which he invited all the commanding officers of regiments, etc.

5th June—At a general court martial, by which a number had been tried for divers crimes, were also tried two followers of the army, one for stealing a horse, and the other for robbing a soldier, and sentenced one thousand lashes each, which were ordered to be put in execution to-morrow the 6th.

7th June—
Head Quarters
Tournay
7th June, 1794

Parole Clebus

His Royal Highness the Duke of York thinks it incumbent on him to announce to the British and Hanoverian troops under his command, that the National Convention of France, pursuing that gradation of crimes and horrors which has distinguished the periods of its government, as the most calamitous of any that has yet occurred in the history of the world, has just passed a decree, that their "soldiers shall give no quarter to the British and Hanoverian troops."

His Royal Highness anticipates the indignation and horror which will naturally arise in the minds of the brave troops whom he addresses, upon receiving this information.

His Royal Highness desires, however, to remind them, that mercy to the vanquished is the brightest gem in a soldier's character; and he exhorts them not to suffer their resentment to lead them to any precipitate act of cruelty on their part, which may sully the reputation they have acquired in the world.

His Royal Highness believes, that it will be difficult for brave men to conceive, that any set of men, who are themselves exempt from sharing in the dangers of war, should be so base and cowardly as to seek to aggravate the calamities of it upon the unfortunate people who are subject to their orders: it was, indeed, reserved for the present time to produce to the world the proof of the possibility of the existence of such atrocity and infamy.

The pretence for issuing this decree, even if founded in truth, could justify it only to minds similar to those of the Members of the National Convention: that is, in fact, too absurd to be noticed, and still less to be refuted; the French must themselves see through the flimsy artifice of a pretended assassination, by which Robespierre has succeeded in procuring that military guard which has at once established him the successor of the unfortunate Louis, by whatever name he may choose to dignify his future reign.

In all the wars which from the earliest times have existed between the English and the French nations, they have been accustomed to consider each other in the light of generous, as well as brave enemies; while the Hanoverians, for a century the allies of the former, have shared in this reciprocal esteem, humanity, and kindness, which have at all times taken place the instant that opposition has ceased; and the same cloak has frequently been seen covering wounded enemies, while indiscriminately conveying to the hospitals of the conqueror.

The British and Hanoverian armies will not believe that the French nation, even under their present infatuation, can so far forget their characters as soldiers, as to pay any attention to a decree, as injurious to themselves as disgraceful to the persons who passed it.

On this confidence his Royal Highness trusts, that the soldiers of both nations will confine their sentiments of resentment and abhorrence to the National Convention alone, persuaded that they will be joined in them by every Frenchman who possesses one spark of honour, or one principle of a soldier: and his Royal Highness is confident that it will only be on finding, contrary to every expectation, that the French army has relinquished every title to the fair character of soldiers and of men, by submitting to, and obeying so atrocious an order, that the brave troops under his command will think themselves justified, and, indeed, under the necessity of themselves adopting a species of warfare for which they will then stand acquitted to their own consciences, to their country, and to the world. In such an event the French army alone will be answerable for the tenfold vengeance which will fall upon themselves, their wives, and their children, and their unfortunate country, already groaning under every calamity which the accumulated crimes of unprincipled ambition and avarice can heap upon their devoted victims.

His Royal Highness desires that this order may be read and explained to the men at three successive roll callings.

10th June—Nothing worth notice occurred till this day; about eleven o'clock, a. m. we were ordered to strike our tents, the baggage to be sent off, and the major part of the army to march in two columns; ours were to be formed at Pont à Chin, on the road between Peck and Courtray. But no movement taking place, we pitched them again about seven o'clock.

14th June—In the afternoon a great deal of thunder and lightning. For some days past the weather has been excessive hot.

18th June—This morning a *feu-de-joie* was fired all round the encampment, from the cannon on the several batteries, in consequence of a victory obtained over the enemy on the Sambre, by the Prince of Orange. The enemy lost 7000 men, twenty-two pieces of cannon, thirty-five ammunition wagons, baggage, stores, etc.

In consequence of some threatening movement of the enemy, about one o'clock, a. m. we struck our tents, and the British light cavalry, infantry and reserve artillery, were ordered to be ready to march at four. About six o'clock we marched from our encampment, leaving the tents packed up, and baggage behind.

We crossed the Scheldt a little below Tournay, and turning to the left, we passed the village of Kain, near the foot of that pleasant place, Mount de la Trinitie, and down along the side of the river through Obigies and Herinne, to a village called Pottes, about fifteen miles from Tournay. We reached this place about midnight, and lay down in the adjoining fields; the weather fortunately was fine.

Throughout our march along the east side of the Scheldt, the prospect is exceedingly delightful, woods, enclosures, fields, and meadows, mixed with the most beautiful variety; every field covered with the finest crops we ever saw, of wheat, barley, rye, flax, etc. and so rich in the soil, that some of the rye stands near eight feet high, and every other species of grain proportionably exuberant.

The iron hand of destructive war has not yet reached this pleasant spot, and on comparing it with the desolated regions which we have lately occupied (though the soil is equally fruitful in both) it would make the most unfeeling heart lament the fatal consequences of war. Wherever we go, the most luxuriant crops are unavoidably destroyed, and the most fertile fields, now in June, assume the dismal prospect of November.

Before the conquering army the affrighted inhabitants fly, frequently leaving their whole dependence behind them, a prey. to the rapacious hand of plunder, which in spite of all order and discipline, too often prevails; anon they return with trembling steps, in hopes to find relief and shelter, when, behold, instead of their once happy cottage, a heap of ruins! All their hopes destroyed for ever, none to pity, none to help!

Let the sympathetic heart draw a picture to itself of their situation.

19th June—At eleven o'clock, a.m. we marched back again by the same route to our former camp ground, at which we arrived about five in the afternoon.

20th June—Last night we lay on the ground without our tents, except a few companies in the brigade. The batt horses which should have followed the army having mistaken the road, and did not arrive till near sun-set this evening. It rained considerably both last night and this morning.

21st June—This evening a little before sun-set, orders were issued for all the heavy baggage of the British to be packed up, and assembled immediately on the left of our line next to Tournay, from whence it was conducted to the other side of the town towards Leuze.

At the same time the Austrian troops left us, being withdrawn to some other quarter.

Our army being thus diminished, it became necessary to contract the line of our encampment, for which purpose our tents were struck after dark, and about one o'clock next morning our new line was formed; the right near the village of Orq, towards the Fauxbourg de Lille; the left reaching the heights near the Orchus road; the British heavy cavalry on the left.

23rd June—This day the heavy baggage set off for Gramont, where it is to be parked till further orders. The bread wagons, etc. are parked without the gate of Tournay, towards the above place. Every imagination is wound up to the highest pitch, in expectation of some great event, from such obvious preparations, but all is doubt and uncertainty. Meanwhile a thousand whimsical stories are circulating every hour among the soldiers.

It is certain, however, that General Clairfait cannot maintain his ground in West Flanders, and that if he gives way, our position here will not be tenable.

24th June—Our suspicions are now confirmed that a retreat is intended, in consequence of General Clairfait's being forced to fall back.

About noon our whole army was in motion, and passing through Tournay, arrived about sun-set at Ronaix, by a very pleasant road. The whole country through which we marched, exhibits a most delightful scene; a pleasing variety of hills and valleys, woods and lawns, the whole covered with the most beautiful verdure, while from the summit of each rising ground you discover a new landscape, above the power of art to describe.

Ronaix is a handsome lively town, has a large market-place, well supplied with cloth, and clothes ready made of all sorts, linen drapery, hardware, toys, etc. with a great number of hogs, which meat is very reasonable here.

It is surrounded, except on the southeast, with hills of a gentle ascent, covered with wood, forming a kind of amphitheatre.

We pitched our camp in two parallel lines, on the south side of the town; the infantry in front, and the heavy cavalry in the rear; the light cavalry on the other side of the town towards Oudenarde. Our out-posts were now along the east side of the Scheldt.

27th June—A heavy cannonading has been heard since day-light toward Oudenarde and beyond.

At noon our tents were struck, baggage packed, and every thing in readiness to march. General Clairfait being attacked by the enemy in three columns, but not prevailing, we pitched our tents again at six o'clock, p. m.

30th June—The enemy has lately bombarded Oudenarde, which is still in our possession, and from whence we have brought our bread, forage, etc. since we have been here.

General Clairfait has fallen back to Ghent.

It is reported the enemy has above three hundred thousand effective men on this frontier, compared with which number all our army is but a small piquet, so that we have begun to retreat; it is probable we may continue to do so, till we find a proper place to make a stand against such unequal numbers.

Some days past have been exceeding sultry, and this evening there fell a little rain, with a great deal of thunder and lightning.

CHAPTER 18

July 1794

3rd July—Agreeable to the orders of yesterday, the tents were struck at two o'clock this morning, and about eight o'clock the whole marched by the right in one column in the following order, *viz*: the British infantry leading in the order of battle, followed by the Hessian infantry; the British cavalry follows the Hessian infantry, and the column is closed by the Hessian cavalry.

About five o'clock, p. m. we reached Gramont, a handsome town situated on the southern declivity of a hill, at the bottom of which flows the river Dender, which, in passing through the town, is divided into two branches, one for navigation, and the other for water-mills, bleaching, etc.

The custom of white-washing the outside of their houses adds greatly to the beauty of the town, which seen from the southward, the houses rising gradually one above the other, has a very pleasant prospect. On the top of the hill is an observatory surrounded by a grove of trees.

The greatest part of our road from Ronaix to Gramont (which was a cross one) was through forests, and over heights of a considerable extent, covered with heath, which is the first barren ground we have seen in this country: which, however, by its variety, was very agreeable, having many exceeding fine prospects over the adjacent country, particularly towards the south-east, where the view was only bounded by the horizon.

4th July—Struck our tents at three o'clock, moved off the ground about seven; the whole of the British marching in one column, the brigade of guards in front.

We pitched our camp near the village of Wambeke, about eight or nine miles to the westward of Brussels.

The country through which we passed this day, is not exceeded in culture or fertility by any we have yet seen. Numberless little hamlets and cottages, shaded with verdant groves, with fields or meadows between, filled with all the luxuriance of nature's bounty, among which are great quantities of hops.

The peasants of both sexes were all busily employed, some reaping, others mowing, all in their several employments; the children homely clad, but strong and hearty, diverting themselves with innocent amusements, form a most complete and finished picture of rural industry, innocence, and happiness.

The weather has been exceeding hot yesterday and to-day, and as we march always in the heat of the day it is very fatiguing for troops carrying so much luggage as the British generally do.

5th July—Halted.

6th July—Marched at five in the morning to Mollem, a village near Asche, which is situated about six miles from Brussels on the *chaussee* to Dendermond, from which it is also six miles.

A column of General Clairfait's army marched through Asche to Brussels this morning, which detained our column for some hours, as they eroded the road before us.

The Austrians have now entirely evacuated West Flanders, with the French, close at their heels.

The Earl of Moira, who has stolen a march with his army by some means or other from Ostend, has reached the Dender, and we hear that some of his rear guard was attacked at Alost this afternoon.

A heavy cannonade has also been heard southward of Brussels all this afternoon. Weather very hot.

7th July—At one o'clock p. m. struck our tents, which, with all the wheel carriages, set off at three, and at nine at night we proceeded in the following order of march, *viz*:

British heavy cavalry with the guns attached to them in the rear.

Brigade of guards
Two twelve-pounders, British
Two howitzers, British
First and second brigades of the line
Two battalions of Hessians
Two twelve-pounders, British
Two howitzers, British
Five battalions, Hessians

8th July—Two battalions of Hessians and the 1st and 8th. dragoon guards to march in the rear, in order to support the rear guard under the command of Major-General Dovey in case of necessity.

In this order marching all night, passing through Brusseghem and Gromberghen; we crossed the great canal leading from Brussels to Antwerp, at Verbrande Brugghe about sunrising, and from thence proceeded through Eppeghem to a village called Semps, where we rested.

The tents, baggage, etc. being sent forward to Waerloos. The fertility of the soil, and the industry of the husbandman still continues through this country, and Ceres smiling amidst her fields loaded with weighty grain, promises a plentiful harvest.

Weather still continues excessive hot.

9th July—This morning before one o'clock we were all under arms, in the order of march of yesterday, crossed the river Senne, a few miles from Semps, and at three o'clock in the morning passed through Malines, which appears to be a fine, well-built town. The main street, which is wide, and ornamented with many elegant buildings, along which is the main road from Brussels to Antwerp, is about a mile long, at each end of which is a lofty gate, adding an air of no small consequence to the town. It is surrounded by a wide deep ditch, and a wall of no great strength, ornamented at small distances with little towers, but the whole much decayed. A fine gravel walk shaded with lofty trees runs all round the rampart, which in summer is very pleasant.

Near the middle of the town is a spacious market-place, on one side of which is the town-hall, and near the other side stands in view the south side of their great church, which is an ancient, Gothic building, with a square tower.

Through the middle of the town flows the river Dyle, over which is a stone bridge with three arches and below it lay several vessels of considerable burthen.

On leaving Malines we kept to the right of the main road, crossing the river Neethe at the village of Duffel; from thence we came across the country to the *chaussee* between Waerloos and Kontigh, (the latter being head quarters) where we encamped, almost smothered with dust. The soil of this country is a light sand, which, in this dry season wherever it is trod upon, the wind raises in clouds like smoke from a furnace, and covers every surrounding object.

This day the army with the Earl of Moira joined us; it still continues to act under his Lordship's command.

Extract from yesterday's orders:

The 3rd dragoon guards will march at half part ten o'clock; they will proceed very slowly along the route of the march of the column, which, it will carefully patrol, obliging all carriages without exception to quit the *chaussee*.

The patrols will apprehend all persons of any nation or denomination whom they may find plundering, or committing any irregularities.

12th July—This evening the enemy, who follow close at our heels, commenced a smart cannonade with our advanced posts, which lasted some hours; but some pieces of cannon, and a reinforcement being sent out, they thought fit to retire to a more convenient distance.

13th July—In the evening came on a storm of thunder and lightning, but not much rain; the latter would be very agreeable at this time, as the ground by reason of the drought is like a heap of ashes. Water being so scarce here we have begun to sink wells, which supply the deficiency tolerably well.

15th July—The enemy are approaching near our out-posts in considerable strength. This morning a brisk fire of musketry was kept up for above two hours by the piquets, etc. after which the enemy retired. Some battalions of Dutch and Hessians being left in the town of Malines, the enemy approached it in the morning, when a heavy cannonade commenced, which continued all day.

16th July—The enemy having possessed themselves of Malines, our troops in front of our portion have yesterday and to-day sent back all their baggage towards Antwerp, which indicate a retrograde movement for the whole. A cannonade has been kept up all this day between the out-posts.

17th July—This day four light companies joined the brigade with a small draught for the Coldstream and 3rd regiment. The light companies joined the flank battalion, which now consists of twelve companies.

The out-posts of each army having established themselves

on their respective sides of the river Neethe, remain very quiet. Weather exceeding sultry.

20th July—Every thing has been very tranquil for some days past.

Whatever enmity may be in the hearts of the rulers of nations or conductors of war against each other, there seems to be little animosity between individuals of the different armies. Since the 17th the advanced posts of the French army have been established on one side of the river Neethe, and our's on the other; the river is about thirty or forty paces wide; the cannon are planted on both sides ready for attack or defence; yet the men walk about, or carefully lay on the bank on each side, and frequently converse with each other. Several of the French have stripped and swam over to our men, bringing with them gin and other liquors, and after drinking with each other with the utmost frankness and cordiality, swim back again to their posts. This familiarity was, however, strictly forbidden as soon as known.

What reflecting mind but must lament the fatal custom, necessity, or other causes, that urge men, not only without remorse, but with an ardent zeal to destroy each other, between whom no cause of complaint ever existed, but only to satiate the ambition, avarice, or revenge of a few individuals.

The flank battalion was divided, the four companies of grenadiers put under the command of Lieutenant-colonel Stanhope, and the eight companies of light infantry under the command of Colonel Sir James Duff.

22nd July—Marched about five o'clock this morning in three columns; our column encamped at Wyneghem, six miles east of Antwerp.

On the road near Antwerp are some very elegant seats of the nobility and gentry; and where we encamped this day is one with a very extensive pleasure ground and gardens, diversified with all the variety of woods, shrubberies, fish ponds, canals, etc. but much out of repair, the proprietor having absconded, perhaps for some political reason.

23rd July—Marched at seven this morning, and about two o'clock encamped near the village of Westwesel, on a vast extended plain covered with heath; on the north side of which our encampment stretched for several miles.

There is no comparison between this country and that we have lately passed through; nothing now is seen but barren heaths, and except what we brought with us, nothing is to be had either to eat or drink; not even water, but what we have out of ditches or ponds.

The magazines of forage, etc. which could not be removed from Antwerp, were set fire to, which burnt all this day.

24th July—Marched and encamped about three miles from Rosendale, eight or nine from Bergen-op-Zoom; Rosendale being our head quarters. Here again are vast plains, hardly half covered with heath, and small patches of wood here and there, which never arrive to any considerable growth; and where there happens to be a cottage, the ground they occupy bears so little, that one would think it hardly repays them for the cultivation.

We dug a great number of wells here, and by that means were pretty well supplied, with water, which, however, in this country is neither plentiful nor good.

29th July—Orders given for the army to march to-morrow morning at four o'clock, in two columns, the heavy baggage being already sent off.

Extract from the orders of the 29th:

For the information of the army, and to prevent disputes, the following is a table of the value of the money in this country:

Dutch Coins

Calculated at the par of eleven Florins Dutch Currency
per Pound Sterling

	Dutch				English	
	Fl	Sti	Doi		s	d
A Dutch ducat worth	5	5	0	Equal to	9	6½
A coin of three florins worth	3	0	0	Equal to	5	5½
A ducatoon worth	3	3	0	Equal to	5	8¾
A deilder worth	1	10	0	Equal to	2	8¾
A coin of twenty-eight stivers worth	1	8	0	Equal to	2	6½
A skillion worth	0	6	0	Equal to	0	6½
A Dutch gilder worth	1	0	0	Equal to	1	9¼
A Dutch rix dollar worth	2	11	0	Equal to	4	6½
A stiver worth	0	1	0	Equal to	0	1

Zealand Coins

A rix dollar worth	2	12	0	Equal to	4	8¾
A half rix dollar worth	1	6	0	Equal to	2	4½
A quarter rix dollar worth	0	13	0	Equal to	1	2¼
One-eighth rix dollar worth	0	6	6	Equal to	0	7
One shilling worth	0	5	6	Equal to	0	6
A double gee worth	0	2	0	Equal to	0	2
A stiver worth	0	1	0	Equal to	0	1

N. B. The foregoing calculation is made as far as the fraction admits of one farthing.

30th July—At half past three o'clock this morning our march was countermanded, and about five we were ordered under arms; immediately after three regiments of light infantry, the brigade of guards, two battalions of Hessian grenadiers, and a few squadrons of other cavalry, marched to the village of Nispen, where we lay under arms a short time, and then advanced about two miles further to a common, where we formed the line of battle. The whole being only considered as a reconnoitring party, the light cavalry advanced in strong patrols to discover the enemy's position; when, in advancing to a high ridge of sand hills, and seeing only a few patrols of the enemy, who retreated upon their approach, they came back again, and soon after we returned to our encampment.

Chapter 19

August 1794

3rd August—
Head Quarters
Rosendale
August 3rd, 1794
The army marches to-morrow morning at half past three o'clock in the following order: the left column to consist of Hanoverian and Hessian cavalry of the 2nd line; Hanoverian and Hessian infantry of the same: two British twelve pounders: Major-General Fox's, and Brigadier-General Graham's brigade: two howitzers: Brigadier-General Balfou's brigade: infantry of the reserve with their guns (*viz.* the brigade of guards:) British cavalry of the 2nd line: Hessian dragoons of the reserve.

The right column was composed similar to the left.

The left column was ordered to march through Etton, and to be under the command of Lieutenant-General Sir William Erskine: the right column through Sprindall, under the command of General Count Walmoden.

4th August—Marched according to the orders of yesterday, and passed through Breda, and encamped near Osterhout, on a large plain full of the vestiges of war. Mounts were thrown up to a great height with excessive labour, and many raised platforms, batteries, redoubts, etc. still retained nearly their original form. Here again we dug wells, and discovered many old ones, which had been filled up with wood, etc. at the bottom not much decayed.

On that part of the common nearest Breda are a great number of criminals hung in chains, four of whom have been lately executed, one broke upon the wheel, and three hung.

One was chained up alive to a high post resembling a crucifix; one chain goes round under his arms, one round his loins, and a third round his ankles; and in that posture it is said that he lived three days, and part of the fourth. I could not learn to any degree of certainty the several crimes of these men.

There are also the remains of a great many more unfortunate wretches scattered up and down this Golgotha; as also the fragments of several wheels and instruments of torture.

Our soldiers were ordered to take down the carcases and bury them, which they did, and burnt the gallows, posts, etc. to which they had been suspended.

Breda is a neat, well built town, strongly fortified, and the Dutch are now busily employed in repairing the works, and making every necessary preparation for a vigorous defence, should the enemy attempt it. The trees of every description are cut down within cannon shot of the town, and every thing removed that might tend to favour the approach of the enemy.

8th August—This day the engineers and others pointed out places for throwing up redoubts, batteries, etc. in front of the encampment, and working parties were ordered accordingly.

18th August—This day John Gorman, a private of the 8th regiment of light dragoons, was shot, pursuant to the sentence of a general court martial, for mutiny. The whole of the British army was under arms on the occasion.

19th August—About three o'clock, p. m. came on a most terrible storm of hail and rain, accompanied with one continued roar of thunder and flames of lightning; it lasted about thirty-five minutes, and set the country all afloat.

23rd August—This day the Prince of Orange visited Breda, and inspected the inundations, which have perfectly well succeeded.

24th August—Early this morning a patrol consisting of 800 cavalry, and 200 infantry, with four pieces of Hessian flying artillery, were lent out to reconnoitre. Upon coming near the village of Tilbourg, they received information that a piquet of 500 French were in it, they accordingly made the necessary arrangements for surrounding the village, but a sergeant of the 16th light dragoons deserting to the enemy, gave them timely notice, by which means they made their escape.

This being the birth-day of the Prince of Orange, a grand entertainment was made at head quarters. In the evening the prince, princess, and several others of their relations, in carriages, viewed the army drawn up at the head of their respective encampments.

28th August—This night at ten o'clock orders were issued to strike the tents immediately, and the army to march at twelve.

29th August—Accordingly we marched soon after twelve, and this afternoon encamped on a wide plain in front of Bois-le-Duc. Marched at four o'clock this morning through Bois-le-Duc, and encamped on some large plains behind it; head quarters being at a village called Udden.

30th August—Bois-le-Duc is a large, beautiful, populous town, strongly fortified both by nature and by art, there being only two roads leading to it, one on the south and the other

136

on the north; these roads are raised with much labour several feet above the level of the meadows through which they pass, near a mile in length; these meadows can be inundated at pleasure; and these passes are so defended, that it is impossible to force them.

31st August—The British infantry were brigaded as follows, taking place the 30th instant:

BRIGADES OF INFANTRY IN THE DUKE OF YORK'S ARMY

First brigade	Major-General Stewart	40th, 55th, 59th and 89th regiments
Second brigade	Major-General Stewart	8th, 27th, 28th and 57th regiments
Third brigade	Major-General Stewart	12th, 33rd, 42nd and 44th regiments
Fourth brigade	Major-General Fox	14th, 37th, 38th and 63rd regiments
Fifth brigade	Major-General Fox	15th, 53rd, 54th and 88th regiments

CHAPTER 20

September 1794

1st September—Head quarters were this day changed to Burlecombe.

14th September—Nothing particular occurred till this day, when the enemy advanced to the eastward of Bois-le-Duc, with a very superior force, seemingly with a design to cut off our retreat; consequently our situation being no longer tenable, this night at eleven o'clock the reserve, consisting of the brigade of guards, and the 3rd brigade of the line, with a proportion of cavalry and artillery, were ordered to march, under the command of that brave and gallant officer Major-General Abercrombie.

15th September—At day-light they began the attack upon the enemy's advanced posts, but without forcing them back; however, it effectually answered the purpose intended of checking their advance, and our troops made a very good retreat back to the camp with very little loss.

16th September—Meanwhile the army was on its march for Graaf, on the river Meufe. The baggage, tents, etc., being sent off in the morning, we marched at midnight, and about four o'clock next morning passed through Graaf, crossed the river Meufe on a pontoon bridge, and encamped at a small distance from the river, to the right, near the village of Wicken, which was head quarters.

Graaf, or Grave, is a small but very strong place, apparently in good repair. The river washes its walls on the north side.

A full allowance of spirits was ordered for the troops this day.

21st September—This day the army marched about five miles further back, and encamped on a hilly common about four or five miles south of Nimeguen.

This situation is very convenient for wet weather, being a dry moorish soil which lays high, but no water to be found near.

The Meufe is now the barrier between us and the French, and had we a little more force, we might defend it; but we are only a handful compared to their multitudes, and they appear to be equally as well appointed in every respect as we are, both cavalry and infantry.

22nd September—The enemy made some attempts to approach the river above Grave, but they were repulsed and lost one piece of cannon.

23rd September—In order to put a stop to that scandalous and too prevalent practice of plundering, his Royal Highness gave this day in public orders a pointed address to the officers of the army, and another caution to the men; at the same time empowering the provost to execute on the spot any one whom he might detect in the commission of that act of disobedience.

A great deal of rain this night, with thunder and lightning.

24th September—This evening the enemy made some advances towards the out-posts of Grave, but they were again repulsed. Very stormy weather.

25th September—This day a spy dressed in the uniform of

an emigrant hussar, was taken up near the camp, as soon as he found himself detected, he swallowed some poison which he had ready prepared. He was conducted to head quarters alive, but although every medical assistance was applied, he died soon after.

26th September—It being discovered that some correspondence has been carried on between some sutlers who follow the camp, and the enemy; an order was issued to apprehend all suspected persons of that description, but nothing of any importance was discovered.

29th September—In consequence of the enemy bringing a great force towards Gennep, and above it, the brigade of guards, the 3rd brigade of the line, a brigade of British light cavalry, and the hussars of Salem, were ordered to march at six o'clock this morning to Gennep, from which place General Abercrombie, with those under his command, removed farther up the river, to communicate, if possible, with the right of the Austrians.

30th September—Several of our officers and those of the French conversed with each other across the river at Gennep, mutually inviting each other to dinner, but which invitation neither party thought proper to accept.

CHAPTER 21

October 1794

1st October—The Austrians under General Clairfait having been defeated, and consequently exposed our left flank uncovered, which the enemy seemed inclined to turn, and being also in great force on our right, near Battenburg, at which place they seem preparing to cross the river; his Royal Highness thought it expedient to contract his army to a more central point, as it was impossible to defend the vast extent which it now occupied.

5th October—Accordingly the principal part of the forces were drawn towards Nimeguen, where a bridge had previously been thrown over the Waal, and the heavy baggage have already passed.

In consequence of this we marched from Gennep at twelve at night through Grosbeck to Nimeguen. The night was extraordinary dark and rainy, and the roads rough and slippery, so that none could walk many yards without stumbling or falling, which made it one of the most toilsome marches we ever met with. About the time we arrived at Grosbeck we discerned day-light appearing, which made every heart ready to sing with Milton, *Hail, holy Light*, etc.

We pitched our tents by the gates of Nimeguen.

Nimeguen is a large, populous town, strongly fortified, standing on a rising ground on the south banks of the river

Waal, and the works have been put in a state of good repair, and are very strong; but there are none towards the river which is large, and runs with a very strong current; but there is a fort on the opposite side.

6th October—At eight o'clock this morning we crossed the Waal, on a bridge of boats, leaving a number of troops behind us to garrison the town of Nimeguen; we marched about seven or eight miles along the dyke, which runs by the north side of the river. These dykes, with which every river in this part of the country is bounded, are raised about twenty feet above the level of the country, with gravel roads on the top, wide enough for two carriages to pass each other. We were cantoned in a number of small villages, and received in general but very indifferent treatment from the inhabitants, who by the bye, if we may judge from appearances, are no friends to us, and give Old England but little thanks for expending her blood and treasure in defending them from the incursions of the Carmagnols, whom they would certainly make more welcome than us: indeed many of them say so to our face, and we have every reason to believe that what they say is true.

A very singular circumstance happened this day, the particulars are as follow:

A few miles before we arrived at our place of destination, from some obstruction in the front among the wagons, the column made a halt for a few minutes, during which time a young lad, a driver, went to a house near the road, and whether he had taken away any thing without paying for it, or from what other cause we knew not, but he was shut out of the house, fired at from the windows, and slightly wounded; several other shots were fired from the windows, and a man of the name of Street, belonging to the 1st regiment, was much wounded and fell. This soon alarmed those who were near, and a crowd of the grenadier battalion assembling

142

round the house, Sergeant Malpas, the drill sergeant of the battalion, was ordered by an officer to go and examine into the matter. He accordingly went, and in forcing the door open broke his sword in half, and following a man up stairs received a stab with a sword in the left breast, upon which he came down, and taking a firelock from a soldier, was going up stairs again, when the man or men above shot him dead on the spot: he fell backwards, and was taken out of the house by those present.

This so enraged the soldiers, that they instantly set fire to the house, which being thatched, in a few minutes was all in a blaze. In the mean time every one was watching to see who should come out of the house. Two men soon jumped out at a window, one of which soon disappeared, the other they seized and instantly hung upon a tree while his house was in flames, and after shooting at, and otherwise mangling him, left him hanging, as a dreadful example to his villainous countrymen.

Two women, one of which had a child in her arms, came out of the house after it was set on fire, and were suffered to go unmolested; the woman who had the child was wounded in the thigh and bled very much.

It was suspected from the firing that was kept up from the windows that there were more than two men in the house, and that they might probably have concealed themselves in the cellars; on that account a sergeant and fifteen men were left at the house during the night, but nothing appeared to confirm that opinion.

This is a very ominous prelude to our winter quarters among the Dutch; however, soldiers are not apt to be superstitious.

7th October—Marched at eight o'clock, passing through Thiel about twenty miles down the river side, and were cantoned at the most convenient places all along the side of the river. The grenadiers of the guards opposite Bommel, the light infantry battalion at Nergnen, Meteron, Aste, etc.; the other battalions of the guards on our left, and the line of British, and Hessians, etc. extending as far up the river side as to communicate with the right of the Austrian army from Emmerick.

12th October—The Dutch troops are on our right as far as Gorcum, etc. and several British troops occupy the district of Bommel. The enemy having got possession of Fort St. Andre by the treachery of the Dutch commander, Lieutenant-General Abercrombie was ordered to retake it, which, he accordingly did, without losing a man: a piquet, consisting of about 400 infantry, with artillery, etc. kept possession of it, and was relieved every forty-eight hours.

Lieutenant-general Abercrombie, who commands in this district, has established his quarters at Bommel.

Head quarters are at Arnheim.

17th October—The grenadier battalion, and two companies of the light infantry, were detached to the post of Heldt, six miles below Bommel, where they remained till the 28th. The enemy are very numerous opposite to us and make some attempts to retake fort St. Andre almost every day. They have thrown some shells into Thiel.

20th October—Yesterday the enemy made a general attack on all the out-posts from Nimeguen. The 37th regiment of foot behaved with great gallantry; but unfortunately mistaking a strong body of French hussars for the hussars of the regiment Rohan in our service, suffered them to enter the village in which they were, when the hussars turning upon them, killed or took prisoners, it is said, all of them, except Major Hope who commanded, and about fifty men.

24th October—This day and yesterday the enemy made a movement towards Nimeguen, which place they seem determined to have, cost what it may.

144

We think it is impossible for them to cross the Waal, if the Dutch stand true to their trust. The whole of the river is commanded by our guns, and batteries erected all along the dyke at convenient distances, besides which, a road is made behind the dyke for guns, carriages, etc. to pass and repass; and the river Waal rolls down in such a torrent, that to construct any thing like a bridge over it, would require much time and trouble.

30th October—A change of position taking place in the army towards our left, the brigade of guards marched at night, so as to occupy the following places an hour before daylight in the morning:

Grenadiers, Wadpnoyin

Light infantry and 1st regiment, Thiel

Coldstream, Yoondon

Third regiment, Sandgate and Echteld

The heavy baggage of the army was ordered to cross the Leck at Wagenigen, to some villages below Rhenen.

31st October—Marched this night, and before daylight took the following cantonments:

Grenadier and light infantry, Dodewaart

First regiment, Heins

Coldstream, Eelft

Third regiment divided between the two last mentioned places.

The French fired several shot at some of our wagons, with sick, etc. which came along the dyke, but did no damage.

CHAPTER 22

November 1794

2nd November—Several shells were thrown into Thiel. A heavy cannonading heard towards Fort St. Andre.

4th November—The cannonading at Fort St. Andre still continues.

5th November—At two o'clock, p. m. our troops made a sortie from Nimeguen, and without firing a shot, entered the enemy's entrenchments, and put all they found to the bayonet. In the mean time the cavalry getting round the flanks, made terrible havoc among the French: it is reported not less than 600 were killed, and a great number wounded, who got away. Prisoners they took none.

General de Burgh commanded, and the troops engaged were the hussars of Damas; British cavalry, 15th light dragoons; infantry, 8th, 27th, 28th, 55th, 63rd, and 78th regiments; with two battalions of Hanoverian infantry, and the Hanoverian *garde du corps*.

6th November—The troops began to evacuate Nimeguen, in consequence of which our brigade again changed its post, in order to make room for them.

The 1st and 3rd regiments to Thiel
Grenadiers to Drumpt

Light infantry to Wadonoyin.

Coldstream to Sandyke.

9th November—Nimeguen was entirely evacuated this day; but the enemy having brought some; guns to bear on the bridge, a random shot cut a rope, by which part of the bridge swung round to the enemy's side, and about 800 Dutch were taken prisoners. The loss would not be great if they were all taken.

13th November—Several regiments having lately joined our army, the whole of the British infantry were brigaded in the following order:

BRIGADES OF BRITISH INFANTRY

First brigade	Major-General Stewart	30th, 40th, 55th, 59th and 79th regiments
Second brigade	Major-General de Burgh	8th, 37th, 44th, 57th and 88th regiments
Third brigade	Major-General Balfour	12th, 33rd, 42nd and 78th regiments
Fourth brigade	Major-General Fox	14th, 38th, 63rd and 80th regiments
Fifth brigade	Major-General Fox	19th, 54th, 84th and 89th regiments
Sixth brigade	Major-General Fox	27th, 28th, 53rd and 85th regiments

The sick have been frequently sent to the general hospitals, totally destitute of necessaries, the fatal consequence of which practice is evident in this severe season.

His Royal Highness, always attentive to the good of the soldiers, issued an order, directing the commanding officers of regiments to pay very particular attention to this object; and likewise ordering the surgeons, purveyors, etc. at the hospitals, to provide them with what is necessary.

17th November—Last night a barn wherein a company of the light infantry was quartered, caught fire, which, with the adjoining house, was consumed. Several articles belonging to the men were destroyed, but no lives lost.

A severe frost set in.

18th November—The enemy having laid siege to Grave, we frequently hear the cannonading there.

21st November—The brigade of guards changed their cantonments again; the grenadiers to Arnheim; 1st regiment to Elden, near Amhun; Coldstream to —— and 3rd regiment to Valburgh.

The light infantry remained on the out-post, and was cantoned at Osterhout, nearly opposite Nimeguen.

There are fourteen British regiments now along the Waal, from Osterhout to Wadonoyin; the Dutch on the right towards Gorcum, and beyond; and Hessians and Hanoverians on the left. There are also five regiments hutted behind Osterhout.

28th November—Working parties from the brigade, of 400 men, daily are employed in completing the defence of the Waal, opposite Nimeguen.

30th November—The frost being gone, the roads (except on the dykes) are so deep as to be almost impassable.

The general rumour now is, of a peace being negotiated, and I think some believe it, but all wish for it.

The number of sick has increased of late in such an extraordinary manner, that above half the number of some battalions are now in the several hospitals.

CHAPTER 23

December 1794

1st December—His Royal Highness has been pleased to order the commanding officers of regiments, on application from their surgeons, to supply the sick with whatever quantity of wine may be necessary.

Last night a tremendous cannonade was kept up at Grave, and with small intervals all this day.

2nd December—Last night we heard no firing from Grave, but some few shots this day. All quiet here.

7th December—The French sentries and our's frequently converse across the river; they complain of having no liquor, and very little meat.

8th December—The sickness still continues among our troops; numbers are sent to the hospitals every day.

The general hospital for the British, which has been at Rhenen for five or six months past, is now crowded, and thirty or forty dying every day.

9th December—Grave still holds out, from whence was heard a very heavy cannonading last night. It is not customary for Dutchmen to stand so much fire.

Our commander in chief being gone to England, the

command of the allied army devolves on Lieutenant-General Count Walmoden, and the British are more particularly under the command of Lieutenant-General Harcourt,

11th December—Early this morning a number of the enemy crossed the river above Nimeguen, on the left of the canal, in some boats, drove back the Hessians, and spiked some pieces of cannon; but a reinforcement arriving, they retreated back again without much loss.

General de Busch, with sixteen rank and file, were killed.

12th December—All is quiet this day, not a single gun to be heard, neither from Grave nor along the Waal.

As a storm is frequently preceded by a calm, so we may expect some work to do soon; flushed with victory, and of an active enterprising spirit, we cannot expect the French will remain long idle.

13th December—The enemy made another attempt to cross the river near the same place as before, but were repulsed.

A heavy firing also at Grave.

14th December—General de Busch was buried with the usual military honours, in the great church at Arnheim.

15th December—A severe frost set in again. The firing at Grave continues.

Every thing remains quiet. Nothing heard from Grave.

22nd December—Sickness still increases.

25th December—Frost continues severe, with a fall of snow.

Meat, and every other article of living is very scarce here, on account of the bridge being broke down at Arnheim by the ice.

28th December—The ice being sufficiently strong in many places to admit infantry to cross, about 700 of the French crossed the Waal at Bommel, and made a lodgement under the dyke, where they continued two days. Some of them penetrated near to Molein, but were driven back again with very little loss. Our loss was two officers wounded, and twelve rank and file killed.

Orders are issued for the sick and heavy baggage of the army to be sent beyond the Leck with all possible expedition.

Several movements took place in order to strengthen the defence of the river towards Thiel and Bommel; the 1st regiment and grenadiers marched to Dodewaart, from whence others moved to Thiel, etc.

29th December—Where is now the boasted security of the Dutch, with all their inundations? Behold the hand of Omnipotence arrests the rapid current; a smooth firm passage, is made over the waves, which all human power and wisdom cannot prevent, and even their chief defence is made subservient to the designs of the enemy.

Frost still continues.

CHAPTER 24

January 1795

1st January—Marched this morning: the grenadiers and light infantry to Dodewaart and Ochton; the 1st regiment to Yssendorn and the 3rd regiment to Echleldt.

The rivers are all completely froze over, and passable at most places.

2nd January—Frost continues excessive severe. Every arrangement is made for a retreat across the Leck; the sick are removing from the general hospital at Rhenen, and every thing indicates a speedy movement; but where we are to make a stand next time, God only knows.

3rd January—Frost still continues, and our sick increase. Duty is, and has been, very hard, and fuel and provisions are very scarce.

4th January—This morning the artillery began to destroy the limbers and carriages of the guns on the several batteries; as all guns, ammunition, etc. that cannot be taken away, are ordered to be destroyed.

7th January—Orders having been previously given, and the cannon and ammunition on the batteries along the Waal being destroyed as much as possible, the army abandoned the post on that river, and crossed the Leck at several places, as previously ordered. The Coldstream and 3rd regiment did not cross that day, for the enemy following up closely, several skirmishes ensued, in which the 3rd regiment had one killed and several wounded. The grenadiers, light infantry, and 1st regiment crossed at Rhenen.

Rhenen is a small town, but pleasantly situated on the north banks of the river Leck; it has no fortification, except a wall and dry ditch, which hardly deserves that name.

It has a small church, with a very high steeple, of a noble appearance and elegant architecture.

Part of the church, and a large building resembling a monastery adjoining, has been converted into an hospital since August last, for the whole of the British army. The hospital, as well as every other place, are filled with soldiers, and no trade of any kind appears. Several large temporary hospitals have been erected in the fields adjoining.

The great mortality which has lately pervaded this army, added to the shameful abuse and neglect in several of the hospital departments, has made it a perfect Golgotha. Upwards of four thousand men having been buried here within the last three months.

At this time near half the army are sick, and the other half much fatigued with hard duty. This is now the tenth day since any of us has had a night's rest, or had time to undress.

8th January—About one o'clock this morning we recrossed the Leck, measures being taken and arrangements made to attack the enemy at Thiel by day-light this morning. But the enemy was beforehand with us, and instead of waiting for us, they attacked General Dundas's out-posts from Burn, etc. and also crossed the Waal at several other places in very great force.

We formed a line in the morning along the dyke on the south side of the Leck. One of our sentries shot an emigrant hussar as he was patrolling in front of our posts, mistaking him for one of the enemy, whose dress his very much resembled.

9th January—Every thing very quiet this day. The army is prodigiously crowded, and the wretched inhabitants greatly distressed, Frost continues severe, with a fall of snow.

10th January—The brigade crossed the Leck a second time, and took our posts on the heights, to the left of Rhenen; sheltered a little in the large sheds used for the purpose of drying tobacco, of which there are great numbers, as that plant is much cultivated here, and seems to thrive well. Frost excessive severe.

11th January—Changed our position to the right of Rhenen, and strong piquets advanced across the Leck. Here also we took shelter in these tobacco sheds, three or four companies in one shed. The sick are removing from the hospital as fast as possible.

12th January—Heard a heavy cannonading on our left towards Arnheim, or beyond. Every thing quiet here.

13th January—Frost still continues.
The manner of burying the dead soldiers here is adapted to the circumstances of the times: in a field appointed for that purpose, a large hole is dug in the ground, from twelve to twenty feet square, more or less, and twelve or fourteen feet deep; here the coffins are piled regularly one above another, from the bottom to within a foot or two of the surface; then they begin another row, complete that to the top, and so on till the hole is full, when they cover the whole over with earth, and then dig another. They are not many days in filling a hole, and the excessive severity of the frost prevents any smell from arising, which otherwise would be intolerable.

I observed on passing by Valenciennes, on the 15th of October, 1793, in our route to Englefontaine, that the inhabitants there had adopted the same method of burying their dead in a place about half a mile distant from the town, only that they always covered the coffin with a little earth before they left it, so that only the side of it could be seen. This might possibly be occasioned by the great mortality which prevailed there at that time, in consequence of the late siege.

14th January—This day the enemy made a general attack on our out-posts on the south side of the Leck, most of which were driven back, while the French appeared advancing in all quarters, especially towards our right, where we had a full view of a column of cavalry and infantry advancing towards the river, but before they reached it, they made a halt. Our piquet opposite Rhenen stood the contest all the afternoon, till darkness put an end to their firing. A few were killed, and Captain Wheatly of the light infantry was wounded, with a number of men.

After dark the piquets were withdrawn, and about midnight the whole army marched by different routes, which had been previously marked out, for the river Yssel, and totally abandoned the Leck, leaving about 250 sick in Rhenen hospital, unable to be moved.

15th January—We marched down to Amoringen, and from thence struck across a common to the villages of Scharpenzaal, Renswort, and Wilderen. The flank battalions occupied Renswort, and close adjoining is a remarkable pleasant seat of some nobleman. We passed by on our march some exceeding strong works, well mounted with cannon, on the line of the inundation between Amersfort and the Rhine; but our night marches having so fatigued us, and the cold so excessive severe, that no prospect could give us any satisfaction, nor was any sight pleasing except a fire.

16th January—The brigade of guards, and Colonel Strutt's brigade of the line were ordered to march at four o'clock and assemble at Lunteron, and await the orders of Major-General de Burgh: we accordingly marched at the appointed hour, and after a very tedious journey, about three o'clock in the afternoon reached the verge of an immense desert, called the Welaw; when, instead of having gained a resting place for the night as we expected, were informed that we had fifteen miles further to go.

Upon this information many began to be much dejected, and not without reason; for several of us, besides suffering the severity of the weather and fatigue of the march, had neither eaten nor drank any thing except water that day.

For the first three or four miles such a dismal prospect appeared as none of us was ever witness to before; a bare sandy desert with a tuft of withered grass, or solitary shrub, here and there: the wind was excessive high, and drifted the snow and sand together so strong, that we could hardly wrestle against it; to which was added, a severity of cold almost insufferable. The frost was so intense, that the water which came from our eyes, freezing as it fell, hung in icicles to our eyelashes, and our breath freezing as soon as emitted, lodged in heaps of ice about our faces, and on the blankets or coats that were wrapped round our heads.

Night fast approaching, a great number, both men and women, began to linger behind, their spirits being quite exhausted, and without hopes of reaching their destination; and if they once lost sight of the column of march, though but a few minutes, it being dark, and no track to follow, there was no chance of finding it again. In this state numbers were induced to sit down, or creep under the shelter of bushes; where, weary, spiritless, and without hope, a few moments consigned them to sleep: but, alas! whoever slept awaked no more; their blood almost instantly congealed in their veins, the spring of life soon dried up; and if ever they

An Officer of the Coldstream Guards

opened their eyes, it was only to be sensible of the last agonies of their miserable existence.

Others, sensible of the danger of sitting down, but having lost the column, wandered up and down the pathless waste, surrounded with darkness and despair; no sound to comfort their ears but the bleak whistling wind; no sight to bless their eyes but the wide, trackless desert and shapeless drift; far from human help, far from pity, down they sink to rise no more!

About half past ten o'clock at night we reached Bickborge, when, to add to our misfortunes, we could hardly find room to shelter ourselves from the weather; every house being already filled with Hessian infantry, who are in no respects friendly to the English. In several houses they positively refused us entrance, and in every one refused us admittance to the fire; at the same time they posted sentries by the cellar doors to prevent the inhabitants from selling us any liquors; even their commanding officer pushed with his own hands a number of our men neck and heels out of his quarters. Thus we were situated, till partly by force, and partly by stealth, we crept in where we could, glad to obtain the shelter of a house at any rate.

17th January—We halted this day, and in the morning wagons were sent out with a number of men to search for those who were left behind. A great number were found dead near the route of the column, but a greater number who had straggled farther off, were never heard of more. In one place seven men, one woman, and a child were found dead; in another, a man, a woman, and two children; in another, a man, a woman, and one child; and an unhappy woman being taken in labour, she, with her husband and infant were all found lifeless. One or two men were found alive, but their hands and feet were frozen to such a degree as to be dropping off by the wrists and ankles.

18th January—Marched at day-light this morning, the grenadiers, 1st Coldstream and 3rd regiments to Vausson. The light infantry battalion, passing Deventer, marched to Welson, six miles below on the banks of the Yssel; the army being cantoned all along the west side of that river from above Zutphen to the sea.

The advanced posts of our part of the army were at Loo and Appledoorn.

Frost still continues.

19th January—Perhaps never did a British army experience such distress as our's does at this time. Not a village nor house but what bears witness to our misery, in containing some dead and others dying; some are daily found who have crawled into houses singly; other houses contain five, six, or seven together, some dead, and others dying, or unable to walk, and as for those that are able, it is no easy matter for them to find their way, for the: country is one continued desert, without roads, and every tract filled up with the drifting and falling snow. Add to all this, the inhabitants are our most inveterate enemies, and where opportunity offers, will rather murder a poor, lost, distressed Englishman, than direct him the right way, several instances of which we have already known. It is reported that in the several columns of the army about 700 are missing, since we left the river Leck.

20th January—Frost continues very severe.

21st January—Our numerous hospitals which were lately so crowded, are for the present considerably thinned. Removing the sick in wagons, without clothing sufficient to keep them warm in this rigorous season, has sent some hundreds to their eternal home; and the shameful neglect that prevails through all that department, makes our hospitals mere slaughter-houses; without covering, without attendance and even without clean straw and sufficient shelter from the weather, they are thrown together in heaps, unpitied, and unprotected, to perish by contagion; while legions of vultures, down to the stewards, nurses and their numberless dependants, pamper their bodies and fill their coffers with the nation's treasure, and like beasts of prey fatten on the blood and carcases of their unhappy fellow creatures; who, of the number that are unhappily doomed to the shades of death, not one in an hundred returns, but perishes under the infernal claws of those harpies, still thirsting for more blood and rioting in the jaws of death.

For the truth of what I say, I appeal to every man in the army who has only for a few hours observed with an attentive eye the general rule of conduct in our hospitals of late, and witness here the scene before me while I now write. A number of men laying on a scanty allowance of dirty, wet straw, which from the heat of their bodies, sends up a visible steam, unable to help themselves; and though a sufficient number of men are liberally paid for their attendance, none has been near for several hours, even to help them to a drink of water. Five carcases, covered only with the rags they wore when they were alive, are piled one upon another in the yard, on pretence that the ground is too hard to bury them until a thaw comes.

This is a very disagreeable subject, but one thing more I must take notice of, which leaves them without excuse.

His Royal Highness has at all times paid great attention to the sick of his army, and directions have been given and regulations made, as circumstances required, tending to promote their comfort and restore their health; besides a number of standing orders, which, if strictly attended to, would remove the greatest part of the prevailing grievances, even at this extraordinary period, one in particular I cannot help taking notice of; it was given out in the order of the 4th of June last, and is as follows:

His Royal Highness the commander in chief directs, that whenever the vicinity of the camp will permit it, a field officer for the week shall be appointed for the inspection of the flying general hospital.

The officer upon this very essential duty is expected to visit frequently the hospital at unstated hours, to superintend the cleanliness and discipline of it in every particular, to examine the diet of the patients, and observe whether they receive that *unremitting care and attention their situation demands*, and to report immediately *any deficiency, neglect or irregularity* to the commander in chief.

An order has also been issued with respect to clothing the sick, which I noticed before; besides the most liberal provision being made for servants or nurses, as well as in apparel, liquor, and every other requisite, leaves no excuse for neglect in those who have the superintending of our now too numerous hospitals.

22nd January—Frost continues severe.

Batt horses, baggage, etc. are sent off, and all sick officers ordered to Lingen, on the banks of the Ems. This is generally the prelude of a march.

26th January—The light infantry left their quarters at Welsen, and marched to Deventer, to relieve General de Burgh's brigade, who are ordered to march to-morrow.

Deventer is a large handsome town, the houses generally commodious, and some elegant. A great number of our stragglers are come in, and many of them having taken the advantage of their absence, have plundered and committed many acts of outrage among the inhabitants in the country through which they have passed. The Dutch and us were no great friends before, but those skulking villains, for whom no punishment is too severe, have given them more cause of hatred and discontent than ever they had before; hence they shut up their shops and deny every thing at our approach, and behold us with a kind of scornful disdain, while they receive the French armies on their approach with acclamations of joy, as their only protectors; for under them their persons are safe, and if their property is taken for the public good, it is punctually paid for with paper.

27th January—Halted at Deventer. The sick sent forward, and a working party employed in destroying the guns and ammunition in the storehouses here; it being a fortified town, the stores are considerable.

29th January—Marched to Hatten, a small village ten miles eastward from Deventer.

30th January—To Pelden, a considerable town on the Regge river; quartered very wide, round among the farm houses.

31st January—To Oldenzaal, one of the Dutch frontier towns towards Germany.

This town is exceedingly distressed on account of so many troops marching through it for two months past, particularly for fuel in this severe season. Their common fuel in this country is peat, which they bring to this town from fifteen or twenty miles distant for the use of the troops. The poor natives are almost starved.

Chapter 25

February 1795

2nd February—Frost, with a heavy fall of snow.

3rd February—All the wagons are employed in removing the stores and ammunition from Delden to Benthem.

4th February—Frost still continues, with frequent falls of snow. The inhabitants, as well as the soldiers, are greatly distressed for want of fuel.

7th February—The French still keep close at our heels; our advanced posts are at Delden, near which place the enemy's patrols occupy.

9th February—A sudden thaw has set in, which lays the country all afloat.

The brigade of guards, except the light battalion, marched for Benthem; the light battalion remaining till relieved by the troops on the advanced post.

10th February—The thaw continuing, the river rose to an amazing height.

The light infantry battalion was relieved this day, and marched for Benthem; the British 16th light dragoons, the hussars of Rohan, Salm's infantry, York rangers, etc. took their post at Oldenzel.

The river between Oldenzel and Benthem being risen to a prodigious height, the light battalion took a circuitous route by Enskedie to Grenowe, where the Hessians being quartered before we arrived, we were quartered round it, at five or six miles distance.

11th February—Marched to Gilhuis, a long village laying under the east side of a ridge of hills, two miles north-west from Benthem, where we remained. The other battalions of the brigade continued their route, the grenadiers to Ippenburen, and the others to Osnaburg, which is head quarters. General Abercrombie, who commands the advanced post, is quartered at Benthem.

13th February—The frost set in again, with a great fall of snow all this day.

The people here are exceeding kind to the English, and have the good will of the soldiers; but the army is much exasperated against the Dutch, for the inhuman treatment we have long experienced among them.

16th February—Frost continues. Our troops keep possession of Oldenzel, Enskedie, etc., and patrols as far as Delden.

17th February—Frost very severe. Notwithstanding the kindness of the inhabitants, outrages and depredations have been already committed here; a proof that no treatment, however kind, will prevent irregularities in the army, if the reins of discipline are slackened.

A woman has been ravished and almost murdered by four of our men, who are discovered, and in confinement.

25th February—Yesterday the light infantry battalion was

ordered to march this morning for Ippenburen, but counter-manded again (except the baggage and sick, which are sent forward) on account of the enemy haying attacked our post at Northorn, a few miles to our right; they were, however, repulsed, and the 57th regiment marched from Benthem this morning as a reinforcement.

Various movements are taking place in our army to strengthen the frontier.

A great number of Dutch soldiers deserted from Holland about this time, and joined our army.

Extract from General Orders:

In paying the army, and making all other payments to be computed in English money, the following coins are to be paid and received, according to the Sterling value expressed opposite their respective, denominations, *viz.*

GOLD	£	s	d
French Louis-d'ors of Louis 15th and 16th	1	0	0
Hanoverian pistole	0	16	8
Frederick d'or	0	16	8
August d'or	0	16	8
Charles d'or	0	16	8
Louis d'ors of Louis 13th and 14th	0	16	8

SILVER	£	s	d
Dutch and German ducats	0	9	5¾
French crowns	0	5	0
Convention thullar	0	4	5¾
Acus	0	3	4
German florins	0	2	2¾

And to prevent misunderstanding tending to disap-pointment with the inhabitants of the country, the army are informed that the following are the general cur-rent coins passing in the Bishopric of Osnaburg, and the rates at which they pass, *viz.*

GOLD	Acus
French Louis-d'ors of Louis 15th and 16th	6
Hanoverian Pistole	5
Frederick d'or	5

August d'or	5	
Carolus d'or	5	
Louis-d'or of Louis 13th and 14th	5	
SILVER	Acus	Marian-Gross
Double and German ducats	2	30
French crowns	1	18
Convention thullar	1	12
Acus	0	36
German florins	0	24

26th February—Marched this morning through Benthem to Scuttorp, a small, ancient looking town, on the river Aa. It has a handsome neat-built church, and a low stone wall round the town. Some of our brigade narrowly escaped drowning as they passed this town, the river having overflowed the road.

Benthem is remarkable for nothing but its castle, an ancient fabric standing on the top of a hill, around which the town is built; the castle contains a range of barracks for the military, but is no way adapted for a modern defence against a powerful enemy. The country around is in general barren, and a ridge of rocky hills runs from Benthem nearly to Scuttorp; on the top of these hills, in a solitary place, is a Jew's burying ground, with several monumental inscriptions.

The inhabitants in general are very good-natured and attentive to the soldiers.

To Rheim, a considerable town on the river Ems; the roads excessive bad, and the weather rainy. Here is a cascade all across the river, made by the dam of some water mills.

28th February—Arrived at Ippenburen, where the grenadier battalion had been for some time. On our march this day we met five regiments of Brunswick going to Benthem, etc. Frost set in again, and the roads excessive heavy.

This town is entirely surrounded by hills, which in summer time must have a very romantic appearance.

Chapter 26

March 1795

4th March—The brigade marched for the following places, being nearer the frontier. The three battalions from Osnaburg to Quakenburg, and the flank battalions to Huschenne, nine miles from Meppen, on the Ems, where General Abercrombie had now established his quarters; they were cantoned this night at Schale, a small straggling village. The roads through which we passed this day were chiefly barren hills.

5th March—To Longerick, a small village.

A great number of troops are moving towards the front from the interior parts of the country.

6th March—Arrived at Hasclunne, a small town on the river Hase. Our regiment of light dragoons overtook us on our march, and continued their route towards Meppen, and the 16th, whom we relieved, has followed the same route. A barren, wild country.

7th March—Halted here. Cold, rainy weather.

8th March—Frost, and a heavy fall of snow. We have miserable quarters here, the people are in general poor, and fuel is very scarce; I saw six Dutch guilders paid for a quantity of peat, not much exceeding a hundred weight.

12th March—Two French prisoners conducted through the town on their way to head quarters, which are still at Osnaburg.

13th March—A patrol, consisting of eight Brunswick hussars, deserted to the enemy, who have taken sixteen men of that corps prisoners.

14th March—A smart skirmish between our advanced posts and those of the enemy a little below Meppen, but without much loss on either side. The two flank battalions are accoutred in their quarters every morning an hour before day-light.

15th March—Our park of artillery is at Vecht, behind Quakenbrugge; they have lately had a supply of 300 horses. It should seem that our army means to defend this place to the utmost, fresh troops are daily arriving from the interior. Frost still severe.

19th March—Last night a colonel of the French, with a flag of truce, came over to Meppen, where Lieutenant-General Abercrombie's quarters are, and this morning passed through Hasclunne on their way to Osnaburg.

20th March—This day two of the inhabitants were robbed by some of our soldiers, and one of them shot through the belly with a pistol. The ball was extracted from his back, but his life is in much danger. A reward of ten guineas is offered by our commanding officers to whoever will bring the guilty to conviction.

21st March—Orders arrived to march to-morrow morning for Quakenbrugge, etc. All the talk is now for England.

22nd March—Marched to Laennegon, about twelve miles distance, a large village pleasantly situated on the river Hase. Weather fine and mild. The country in general barren heaths.

23rd March—To Quakenbrugge, distance about eleven miles. There are some cultivated spots and woods near the rivers, which in summer are very pleasant.

This is a fine large town situated on the same river; they seem to have suffered but very little by the war; but they charge the English an exorbitant price for every article. They appear to be all Roman Catholics in this part of the country, from the relics of superstition set up at every public place.

As we entered the town, we met some religious processions, in a peculiar dress, both men and women of all ages.

The people in town behaved very kind to the soldiers in their quarters.

24th March—Marched at seven this morning to Vecht, a small town, but pretty regular in its buildings. It has a large church, tolerably well ornamented.

The gable end of the houses throughout all this country are generally next the street, and in the common houses contains all the windows in the house.

Many large farm houses, and all the cottages in the country, have no chimneys; a few boards are placed above the fire to prevent the sparks from flying up to the thatch, and the smoke is left to find its way out how it can. Sometimes a hole is made for that purpose at one end of the ridge, and sometimes not; and in the country places their dwelling, their barn, cow-house, and stable are all in one. You enter by a great door at the end of the house, large enough to admit a wagon loaded with corn; on the right and left, close to the walls, stand properly arranged, the cows, horses, or other animals, with their heads towards the centre of the house, over them is piled their corn, straw, etc., the space in the middle is for threshing.

On the floor at the farther end is the fire, and many have their beds almost resembling playhouse boxes, some with sliding and others with folding doors, ranged along each side.

In all the towns and villages here, one ill-looking custom prevails, that is, every house has a dunghill before the door, in that part of the street where the pavement for foot passengers is in England, so that we can seldom get into any house without walking over heaps of dung. The people in general behave with great kindness to our troops, especially where they are civilly treated by them, which does not always happen.

25th March—Halted. Weather fine and mild.

The park of artillery which has been here some time, is moving off, but the roads are so excessive bad, that the heavy pieces as yet remain immoveable. Part of the artillery and ammunition is to be left with those troops that remain.

26th March—Marched to Wildhausen. This is a regular but a small town, standing on the west side of the river Lette. A rampart of a considerable height made of earth, with a dry ditch, runs round the town, except the east side, which is washed by the river, on which several water-mills are built. The ditch and ramparts are covered with stately trees, which make an agreeable shady walk.

Observed a number of women digging in the garden round this place.

27th March—Marched to a small straggling village called Leeste, about six miles from Bremen. The other three battalions marching into Bremen. The country through which we passed this day is in general a barren waste.

28th March—The two flank battalions marched into Bremen, where our brigade was quartered. The head quarters were also here, and the several departments which accompany it.

Bremen being a free town, upon the approach of the army claimed its privilege as neuter with respect to the war, and objected to having any troops quartered on them; but finding it was in vain to contend, they at last consented, and received first two regiments of Hanoverians, and then the brigade of guards. The other troops all marched through without halting. It is a large, rich, and handsome town, situated on the river Wesser, about sixty miles from the sea. The river here is navigable only for small craft. The town is tolerably well fortified, with high ramparts and a wet ditch; several cannon are mounted round the town, but as war is their aversion, they pay but little, attention to the slate of the works.

They have troops of their own which mount guard at the different posts, and several other places in town, where regular and proper guard rooms are built. This corps consists of about 600 men, divided into six companies, they are clothed in a red uniform, turned up with white; they have large red cloaks for cold or wet weather. The expense of the whole amounts to about 6500 pounds per annum.

The country round here is generally low, therefore liable to inundation.

Over the river is a wooden bridge, along the lower side of which is formed a range of corn-mills, thirteen in number, all across the river; they are constructed so as to float, and rife and fall with the water, and each of them can be moved at pleasure, with all its apparatus, with as much facility as a barge.

From an ingenious mechanism placed here also, the town is plentifully supplied with water.

The several streets, and the houses along the river side, have a fine appearance; the ends of the houses, which always front the streets or other public places, being variously ornamented with painting, carving, plaster, etc.

There is a public cellar under the townhouse, in which are some remarkable large butts for holding beer and other liquors, which are viewed as a curiosity.

The officers and soldiers were quartered promiscuously, as the burgher's names came to hand, and many a soldier had far more elegant apartments than his captain.

The behaviour of the people to us was remarkably kind and polite. It is something like a dream or fairy vision, and we could hardly give credit to our own senses; we who had lately been so buffeted about by fortune and the French, driven like vagabonds through frost and snow, over all the wilds of Holland, and who in our greatest extremities, when we asked for any thing to refresh ourselves, with the money in our hands, was answered only with a shrug up of the shoulders, nix nix, nix bread, nix butter, nix beer, nix brand-wyn for the Englishman. Now to be seated in the most elegant apartments, servants attending ready to anticipate every wish; beds of the softest down to repose upon, without being disturbed in the morning with the thundering of cannon, or the usual alarms of war; it seemed like some sudden enchantment, but it proved real, for they used us like part of their own family, or children which had been long absent, and now returned, and omitted nothing that could contribute either to our ease or pleasure.

29th March—The brigade attended divine service at one of the churches.

30th March—Every preparation is making for the embarkation of all the British infantry. A small detachment of artillery to be left with the cavalry, who are to remain. Several regiments passed through on their way for Bremen Lake, to embark.

31st March—We here see the genuine advantages of trade and commerce, and the inestimable, blessings of peace; here poverty hides her pallid face, and plenty, the fruits of industry, smiles on all around.

Several regiments pass through every day, and every preparation is making for our embarkation. We remain here till all the other regiments are past.

The four grenadier companies joined their respective battalions on the 18th inst. There now remains four battalions in our brigade.

CHAPTER 27

April 1795

9th April—The brigade of guards were ordered to march, and the following routes appointed for them, *viz*:

The flank battalion and 1st battalion of the 1st regiment of guards, to march, on the 10th inst. to Beverstadt, etc. by the following route: Friday, April 10th—Ofterholtz, Schambeek, Penningbuttle, and environs. Saturday, April 11th—Beverstadt, Stemmen, Ostendorf, and environs.

The Coldstream and 3rd regiment to march April 11th, to Hagen, etc. by the following route: Saturday, April 11th—Mayemberg, Schavanwede. Sunday, April 12th—Hagan, Calsbruke, Bramstadt, Wilstadt. To remain till farther orders.

The undermentioned general officers to take the command of the following regiments and corps:

Major-General Moorhead	9th. Royal artillery, Royal military artificers. Light infantry, First regiment, Coldstream regiment, Third regiment of guards, Corps of royal wagoners
Hon. Major-General de Burgh	Twelfth regiment, 27th, 28th, 40th, 54th, 57th, 59th, 79th, 80th, 84th, and the loyal emigrants
Major-General Gordon	Third regiment buffs, 14th, 19th, 33rd, 38th, 42nd, 53rd, 63rd, 78th, and 88th
Major-General Coates	Eighth regiment foot, 37th, 44th, 55th, 85th, and 89th

10th April—The light infantry and 1st regiment marched according to the orders of yesterday, distance about fifteen miles. The country in general is a light sandy soil, and more fruitful than that we have lately passed through.

From about Osterholtz there is a most beautiful prospect towards Bremen. The principal buildings, churches, spires, etc. of Bremen are plainly seen terminating the view; and between is an extensive lake, in which are a great number of islands, filled with groves of trees, houses, churches, etc. the whole forming a most delightful landscape.

The greatest part of our soldiers left Bremen with much regret. The generous and elegant entertainment we met with there, far surpassed any thing we ever experienced before, and I may venture to say, ever will again. A great number accompanied us out of town, and showed every possible respect. Several female heroines took leave of their friends and followed us.

11th April—Marched to Beverstadt, a village about fifteen miles distance; the country rather barren. The village being small, we were much crowded.

12th April—Halted there

13th April—To Wilderstadt, a village near the river side, a few miles above Bremen Lake.

14th April—Embarked at five o'clock in the morning, at the mouth of the creek near Bremen Lake, on board the following transports:

LIGHT INFANTRY

Ships	Number of men
Ann	303
Briton	300

176

First Regiment

Richard	360
John	160
Alexander	270

Coldstream

Bellona	320
Loyal Briton	250

Third Regiment

Albion	340
Three Brothers	230

The troops on hoard each ship were divided into three watches; one of which was always upon deck, night and day, on account of the ship's being so much crowded.

18th April—Last night an artillery-man fell overboard one of the transports and was drowned.

20th April—Weighed anchor and attempted to drop down the river, but the wind failing cast anchor again.

21st April—Weighed anchor and fell down to the opening of the river; anchored again; wind south-west.

22nd April—This day all the fleet, except a few, dropt down near the mouth of the river and lay at anchor, waiting for the others coming down. The whole fleet with the convoy was upwards of 200 sail. The river here, including the tracts of sand which the tide covers at high water, is fifteen miles wide; but the road for ships of burthen is narrow and crooked, marked with buoys on each side; those on the right, white; those on the left, black.

23rd April—Last night we had a heavy squall of wind, but no damage was done.

24th April—The fleet sailed, and about dusk cleared, the mouth of the Wesser, wind south-west. In the river we saw the mast of a transport which was lost three months ago by going out of the tract.

25th April—Continued under a brisk gale on the larboard tack, close to the wind all day; the gale stronger towards night.

26th April—Last night and early this morning it blew what we fresh water sailors thought a perfect hurricane; the sea went mountains high, and exhibited such a scene as few of us had ever witnessed before. The soldiers whose turn it was to be on deck were forced to remain below, the sea breaking frequently over the ship with such violence that we thought we were going to the bottom; so that between sea-sickness and the storm we were in a very uncomfortable situation: but in the forenoon the wind much abated, but not much our sickness, which was almost universal.

27th April—Kept upon the same tack all this day, being driven a great way to the northward by the storm yesterday morning. The fleet which had been scattered very wide by the storm collected itself closer together; we believe none suffered much damage; the *Three Brothers*, in which part of the 3rd regiment was, lost her bowsprit and part of her head.

30th April—This day we had the pleasure of be holding British ground once more, which proved to be Cheviot hills, and the high ground to the northward of them. The sea sickness began to abate, and a kind of secret joy brightened every countenance, in hopes of soon reaching our native country, and ending our tedious voyage.

Chapter 28

May 1795

1st May—Kept beating up against the wind, but made very little way. Passed Banbury Castle, distance two leagues.

2nd May—Wind veered a little more to the east, by which we were enabled to reach off Whitby before sun-set. This day we passed in sight of Shields, Sunderland, etc. The shore on the Yorkshire coast is generally high and rocky.

Whitby, with some other towns along that shore, are curiously built under the shelter of the cliffs and hills, so that hardly a house can be seen, till you are close upon them. We came along near the shore with a gentle breeze, and fine sun-shine. The shore, as far up as Flamborough Head, is high steep rocks, inhabited by numberless flocks of seagulls, and other sea birds.

3rd May—Last night a calm and thick fog coming on, we were forced to cast anchor, and this morning made a little way, but the coast being dangerous, and the fog continuing all day, we anchored again, and remained till next morning.

4th May—Found ourselves off Cromer in Norfolk, distant four miles. The morning clear and a brisk gale, but directly against us. Weighed anchor and made a little way, the tide also coming strongly against us. About eleven o'clock, a. m. cast anchor with the fleet.

5th May—Weighed anchor, and with the principal part of the fleet reaching off Yarmouth, anchored in the roads. Weather very fine and calm.

Yarmouth presents a fine prospect: from the roads, the houses all built with brick, and covered with tiles, appear of a red colour; but the great church and one chapel are the only buildings which appear any way conspicuous.

6th May—Weighed anchor at day-light, and proceeded with a fresh gale within sight of the shore, but a calm succeeding, and night coming on, the fleet anchored. The divisions of the fleet parted this day, that for Portsmouth standing off to the left, and that for Harwich putting in there.

7th May—Weighed anchor at day-light, and with a gentle breeze passed the Nore, and anchored at Gravesend.

8th May—Weighed anchor about ten a. m. and with a brisk gale arrived at Greenwich.

This morning three companies of the 1st regiment disembarked, were seen by his Majesty, and marched to London.

9th May—The remainder of the brigade disembarked at seven o'clock this morning, and marched to the parade in St. James's Park, from whence each battalion marched to their several quarters.

The men had eight days leave given them, excused from all kinds of duty, in order to see their friends.

* * * * * * * *

Thus ended our expedition, which, though unsuccessful in the end, all the nation will be ready to allow was not owing either to a want of courage or conduct in the officers or men engaged in it, but to a number of events which could neither be foreseen or prevented; such as the extraordinary exertions of the enemy, such, indeed, as neither they nor any other nation could continue for any considerable time. The freezing of the Waal, which does not happen to such a degree perhaps once in a century; and at the same time the raging sickness which prevailed, reduced our army to less than half its former number.

Under all these circumstances, it is rather to be wondered at that we effected such a safe retreat, especially through a country, whose inhabitants, as far as they durst avow themselves, were as much, or more our enemies, than the French.

* * * * * * * *

As various reports have been circulated concerning the donation articles which our generous friends in England, Scotland, and Ireland, subscribed for and sent us, the following is nearly the proportion that each man received who was present with his regiment at all the different times of delivery, during the time we were on the continent.

Blue cloth trousers, for which we paid 2s. each	one pair
Great coats	one
Flannel waistcoats	three
Flannel drawers	two pair
Flannel socks	two pair
Flannel nightcaps	one
Shoes	four pair
Stockings	two pair
Handkerchiefs	one
Gloves	two pair

The women and children also who were present with us in the month of March, 1794, received each a proportion of things, such as grey cloaks, flannel shifts, petticoats, shoes, children's caps, and other flannel articles.

Several of the above articles, the shoes in particular, were of the best quality and workmanship, and were of infinite service to us, especially in a country where the materials for making them are so very bad.

Our soldiers frequently broke out in rough, but sincere

expressions of gratitude to those benevolent characters who so generously and timely supplied our wants; especially to the ladies, several of whom we were informed by the papers, disdained not to make up with their own fair hands, a number of the articles which we received.

LEONAUR

ALSO FROM LEONAUR

AVAILABLE IN SOFTCOVER OR HARDCOVER WITH DUST JACKET

WELLINGTON AND THE PYRENEES CAMPAIGN VOLUME I: FROM VI-TORIA TO THE BIDASSOA *by F. C. Beatson*—The final phase of the campaign in the Iberian Peninsula.

WELLINGTON AND THE INVASION OF FRANCE VOLUME II: THE BIDAS-SOA TO THE BATTLE OF THE NIVELLE *by F. C. Beatson*—The second of Beatson's series on the fall of Revolutionary France published by Leonaur, the reader is once again taken into the centre of Wellington's strategic and tactical genius.

WELLINGTON AND THE FALL OF FRANCE VOLUME III: THE GAVES AND THE BATTLE OF ORTHEZ *by F. C. Beatson*—This final chapter of F. C. Beatson's brilliant trilogy shows the 'captain of the age' at his most inspired and makes all three books essential additions to any Peninsular War library.

NAVAL BATTLES OF THE NAPOLEONIC WARS *by W. H. Fitchett*—Cape St.Vincent, the Nile, Cadiz, Copenhagen, Trafalgar & Others

SERGEANT GUILLEMARD: THE MAN WHO SHOT NELSON? *by Robert Guillemard*—A Soldier of the Infantry of the French Army of Napoleon on Campaign Throughout Europe

WITH THE GUARDS ACROSS THE PYRENEES *by Robert Batty*—The Experiences of a British Officer of Wellington's Army During the Battles for the Fall of Napoleonic France, 1813.

A STAFF OFFICER IN THE PENINSULA *by E. W. Buckham*—An Officer of the British Staff Corps Cavalry During the Peninsula Campaign of the Napoleonic Wars

THE LEIPZIG CAMPAIGN: 1813—NAPOLEON AND THE "BATTLE OF THE NATIONS" *by F. N. Maude*—Colonel Maude's analysis of Napoleon's campaign of 1813.

BUGEAUD: A PACK WITH A BATON *by Thomas Robert Bugeaud*—The Early Campaigns of a Soldier of Napoleon's Army Who Would Become a Marshal of France.

TWO LEONAUR ORIGINALS

SERGEANT NICOL *by Daniel Nicol*—The Experiences of a Gordon Highlander During the Napoleonic Wars in Egypt, the Peninsula and France.

WATERLOO RECOLLECTIONS *by Frederick Llewellyn*—Rare First Hand Accounts, Letters, Reports and Retellings from the Campaign of 1815.

AVAILABLE ONLINE AT
www.leonaur.com
AND OTHER GOOD BOOK STORES
NAP-2

LEONAUR

ALSO FROM LEONAUR

AVAILABLE IN SOFTCOVER OR HARDCOVER WITH DUST JACKET

THE JENA CAMPAIGN: 1806 *by F. N. Maude*—The Twin Battles of Jena & Auerstadt Between Napoleon's French and the Prussian Army.

PRIVATE O'NEIL *by Charles O'Neil*—The recollections of an Irish Rogue of H. M. 28th Regt.—The Slashers— during the Peninsula & Waterloo campaigns of the Napoleonic wars.

ROYAL HIGHLANDER by *James Anton*—A soldier of H.M 42nd (Royal) Highlanders during the Peninsular, South of France & Waterloo Campaigns of the Napoleonic Wars.

CAPTAIN BLAZE *by Elzéar Blaze*—Elzéar Blaze recounts his life and experiences in Napoleon's army in a well written, articulate and companionable style.

LEJEUNE VOLUME 1 by *Louis-François Lejeune*—The Napoleonic Wars through the Experiences of an Officer on Berthier's Staff.

LEJEUNE VOLUME 2 by *Louis-François Lejeune*—The Napoleonic Wars through the Experiences of an Officer on Berthier's Staff.

FUSILIER COOPER *by John S. Cooper*—Experiences in the 7th (Royal) Fusiliers During the Peninsular Campaign of the Napoleonic Wars and the American Campaign to New Orleans.

CAPTAIN COIGNET *by Jean-Roch Coignet*—A Soldier of Napoleon's Imperial Guard from the Italian Campaign to Russia and Waterloo.

FIGHTING NAPOLEON'S EMPIRE by *Joseph Anderson*—The Campaigns of a British Infantryman in Italy, Egypt, the Peninsular & the West Indies During the Napoleonic Wars.

CHASSEUR BARRES by *Jean-Baptiste Barres*—The experiences of a French Infantryman of the Imperial Guard at Austerlitz, Jena, Eylau, Friedland, in the Peninsular, Lutzen, Bautzen, Zinnwald and Hanau during the Napoleonic Wars.

MARINES TO 95TH (RIFLES) by *Thomas Fernyhough*—The military experiences of Robert Fernyhough during the Napoleonic Wars.

HUSSAR ROCCA by *Albert Jean Michel de Rocca*—A French cavalry officer's experiences of the Napoleonic Wars and his views on the Peninsular Campaigns against the Spanish, British And Guerilla Armies.

SERGEANT BOURGOGNE by *Adrien Bourgogne*—With Napoleon's Imperial Guard in the Russian Campaign and on the Retreat from Moscow 1812 - 13.

AVAILABLE ONLINE AT
www.leonaur.com
AND OTHER GOOD BOOK STORES

NAP-3

LEONAUR

ALSO FROM LEONAUR

AVAILABLE IN SOFTCOVER OR HARDCOVER WITH DUST JACKET

A JOURNAL OF THE SECOND SIKH WAR by *Daniel A. Sandford*—The Experiences of an Ensign of the 2nd Bengal European Regiment During the Campaign in the Punjab, India, 1848-49.

LAKE'S CAMPAIGNS IN INDIA by *Hugh Pearse*—The Second Anglo Maratha War, 1803-1807. Often neglected by historians and students alike, Lake's Indian campaign was fought against a resourceful and ruthless enemy-almost always superior in numbers to his own forces.

BRITAIN IN AFGHANISTAN 1: THE FIRST AFGHAN WAR 1839-42 by *Archibald Forbes*—Following over a century of the gradual assumption of sovereignty of the Indian Sub-Continent, the British Empire, in the form of the Honourable East India Company, supported by troops of the new Queen Victoria's army, found itself inevitably at the natural boundaries that surround Afghanistan. There it set in motion a series of disastrous events-the first of which was to march into the country at all.

BRITAIN IN AFGHANISTAN 2: THE SECOND AFGHAN WAR 1878-80 by *Archibald Forbes*—This the history of the Second Afghan War-another episode of British military history typified by savagery, massacre, siege and battles.

UP AMONG THE PANDIES by *Vivian Dering Majendie*—An outstanding account of the campaign for the fall of Lucknow. *This is a vital book of war as fought by the British Army of the mid-nineteenth century, but in truth it is also an essential book of war that will enthral military historians and general readers alike.*

BLOW THE BUGLE, DRAW THE SWORD by *W. H. G. Kingston*—The Wars, Campaigns, Regiments and Soldiers of the British & Indian Armies During the Victorian Era, 1839-1898.

INDIAN MUTINY 150th ANNIVERSARY: A LEONAUR ORIGINAL

MUTINY: 1857 by *James Humphries*—It is now 150 years since the 'Indian Mutiny' burst like an engulfing flame on the British soldiers, their families and the civilians of the Empire in North East India. The Bengal Native army arose in violent rebellion, and the once peaceful countryside became a battleground as Native sepoys and elements of the Indian population massacred their British masters and defeated them in open battle. As the tide turned, a vengeful army of British and loyal Indian troops repressed the insurgency with a savagery that knew no mercy. It was a time of fear and slaughter. James Humphries has drawn together the voices of those dreadful days for this commemorative book.

AVAILABLE ONLINE AT
www.leonaur.com
AND OTHER GOOD BOOK STORES

SC-1

LEONAUR

ALSO FROM LEONAUR

AVAILABLE IN SOFTCOVER OR HARDCOVER WITH DUST JACKET

WAR BEYOND THE DRAGON PAGODA by *J. J. Snodgrass*—A Personal Narrative of the First Anglo-Burmese War 1824 - 1826.

ALL FOR A SHILLING A DAY by *Donald F. Featherstone*—The story of H.M. 16th, the Queen's Lancers During the first Sikh War 1845-1846.

AT THEM WITH THE BAYONET by *Donald F. Featherstone*—The first Anglo-Sikh War 1845-1846.

A LEONAUR ORIGINAL

THE HERO OF ALIWAL by *James Humphries*—The days when young Harry Smith wore the green jacket of the 95th-Wellington's famous riflemen-campaigning in Spain against Napoleon's French with his beautiful young bride Juana have long gone. Now, Sir Harry Smith is in his fifties approaching the end of a long career. His position in the Cape colony ends with an appointment as Deputy Adjutant-General to the army in India. There he joins the staff of Sir Hugh Gough to experience an Indian battlefield in the Gwalior War of 1843 as the power of the Marathas is finally crushed. Smith has little time for his superior's 'bull at a gate' style of battlefield tactics, but independent command is denied him. Little does he realise that the greatest opportunity of his military life is close at hand.

THE GURKHA WAR by *H. T. Prinsep*—The Anglo-Nepalese Conflict in North East India 1814-1816.

SOUND ADVANCE! by *Joseph Anderson*—Experiences of an officer of HM 50th regiment in Australia, Burma & the Gwalior war.

THE CAMPAIGN OF THE INDUS by *Thomas Holdsworth*—Experiences of a British Officer of the 2nd (Queen's Royal) Regiment in the Campaign to Place Shah Shuja on the Throne of Afghanistan 1838 - 1840.

WITH THE MADRAS EUROPEAN REGIMENT IN BURMA by *John Butler*—The Experiences of an Officer of the Honourable East India Company's Army During the First Anglo-Burmese War 1824 - 1826.

BESIEGED IN LUCKNOW by *Martin Richard Gubbins*—The Experiences of the Defender of 'Gubbins Post' before & during the sige of the residency at Lucknow, Indian Mutiny, 1857.

THE STORY OF THE GUIDES by *G.J. Younghusband*—The Exploits of the famous Indian Army Regiment from the northwest frontier 1847 - 1900.

AVAILABLE ONLINE AT
www.leonaur.com
AND OTHER GOOD BOOK STORES

SC-2

Lightning Source UK Ltd.
Milton Keynes UK
UKOW01f1952220217
295098UK00001B/20/P